JAPAN FOR

D0253133

JAPAN
FOR
STARTERS

52 Things You Need to Know About Japan

Text and Illustrations by
Charles Danziger

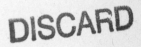

KODANSHA INTERNATIONAL
Tokyo • New York • London

Originally published as The American Who Couldn't Say Noh.

Published by Kodansha International Ltd., 17–14 Otowa
1-chome, Bunkyo-ku, Tokyo 112, and Kodansha America, Inc.

Distributed in the United States by Kodansha America, Inc.,
114 Fifth Avenue, New York, New York 10011, and in the
United Kingdom and continental Europe by Kodansha
Europe Ltd., 95 Aldwych, London WC2B 4JF.
Printed in Japan. First edition, 1993.
First paperback edition, 1996.
10 9 8 7 6 5 4 3 2 1
99 98 97 96

LCC 93–23986
ISBN 4–7700–2087–2

CONTENTS

II THE BUSINESS WORLD

III THE TRADITIONAL WORLD

Introduction

One fine autumn day I found myself transplanted from a tiny Manhattan apartment to an even tinier room in a student dormitory in Nagoya, Japan. My arrival at the dorm prompted my new Japanese dorm-mates to call an emergency meeting—without me—to decide how to deal with the first *gaijin*, or foreigner, ever to darken their doorstep. The posting at the real estate agency had, after all, clearly stated NO FOREIGNERS ALLOWED, but, luckily for me, the sign was in Japanese (which I could not read) and the kindly landlord was willing to give me a chance. I tried to win the friendship of my new dorm-mates with the promise of free lodgings in New York City should ever the need arise (an empty offer at the time, though six years and eighteen tours of New York later they are still taking me up on it), and it must have worked because in a few short weeks they had recovered from the shock of my presence and we became the best of friends.

In those early days, I quickly mastered such basics as how to air out a futon; how to cook communal late-night "hot pots" of fish, vegetables, and tofu; and how to use a squat toilet. I also learned to stop panicking when the phone rang and I was expected to converse using a vocabulary largely limited to *moshi moshi*—the phrase for "hello." Some of the happiest days of my life were spent in Nagoya studying Japanese intensively at Nanzan University, a marvelous intellectual boot camp fully equipped with a high-tech language laboratory that looked like something straight out of the command center of the *Starship Enterprise*.

After returning home from Nagoya and working for a year on Wall Street, I decided to move once again to Japan—this time to Tokyo—to join a large Japanese law firm. My first day of work set the tone for what proved to be a crash course in Japanese business etiquette. I went around to the Japanese lawyers (who were addressed as *sensei*, meaning "teacher"), bowed, and asked each in turn for his or her "humble consideration in the future." I then settled down to an unforgettable year marked by client meetings held in Japanese (my electronic Japanese-English dictionary was never far from my side), late nights spent crooning with colleagues at local *karaoke* "sing-along" bars, business trips that included overnight stays in coffin-size capsule hotel beds, and more lunches than I care to recall featuring eel, dried seaweed, pickles, and rice. And then there was the time when three of my co-workers and I donned asbestos suits, sailed in a small boat to a chemical tanker anchored off the coast of Kobe, literally jumped on board the vessel unannounced in front of the hostile crew, and, armed with the appropriate seizure papers, arrested the ship on the spot. But this is the subject of another book.

The pages that follow contain my accounts of some of what I experienced of everyday life in Japan, whether it be talking vending machines, business card etiquette, or blowfish cuisine.

I have tried to sum up the essence of my experiences in short sketches, each one focusing on some distinctive feature of Japan. The essays fall into three groups: modern life, business, and tradition. I concentrated on those aspects that I believe are characteristic of Japanese life—and which for me were the most fun to relive. I hope the information here will guide unwitting foreigners through Japan's potential perils and pleasures.

Finally, a note about the drawings in this book. They are mine. And like the essays, they are intended to intrigue and encourage the reader to learn more about Japan, a country for which I feel great affection.

Charles Danziger
New York

NOTE ON PRONUNCIATION

JAPANESE	EQUIVALENT
a	as in f<u>a</u>ther
e	as in p<u>e</u>n
i	as in f<u>ee</u>t
o	as in c<u>oa</u>t
u	as in m<u>oo</u>d

Double vowel sounds such as "aa," "ii," and "oo" are pronounced in the same manner as their singular counterparts but are held for an extra beat. Thus the word for company president, *shachoo*, is pronounced *sha-cho-o*. Mixed double vowels such as "ei" and "ae" are not diphthongs, but carry the sounds of the individual vowels, again making two syllables.

I

the
MODERN
WORLD

Barely Room for Teddy

CAPUSERU HOTERU

capsule hotel

Like a cramped combination of cocoon, couchette, and coffin, Japan's "capsule hotel" represents a revolution in economical, space-saving lodgings. Rooms are a thing of the past in this honeycomb-designed hotel, where each guest sleeps encased in an individual body-size capsule.

Not for those easily prone to claustrophobia (or suffocation), the average capsule measures 3 $^1/_2$ feet high, 3 $^1/_2$ feet wide, and 7 feet long, so there's barely room for teddy. Reflecting the Japanese skill in miniaturizing just about anything, each capsule is fully equipped with comforter, pillow, air conditioner, clock radio, night light, wall shelf, and, at the foot of the capsule, color TV and video. After soaking in the hotel's public bath, the occupant crawls headfirst into the capsule, zips up the module's exposed end, and beds down alongside rows and rows of other capsules like the proverbial bug in a rug. When the lights go out, the place is transformed into a settlement of snoring sushi rolls.

With taxis to the city suburbs

running into the hundreds of dollars and trains generally stopping around the witching hour of midnight, the inexpensive capsule hotel offers a reasonable alternative for male night owls who don't want to pay the earth to get home. (Women are generally excluded from capsule quarters unless they are with their mates.) The Central Inn capsule hotel describes itself as "Near the station. Twenty-four hours OK. Peaceful, clean, and economical. Useful for tomorrow." America's Holiday Inn, eat your heart out.

For insomniac businessmen who just can't quit, there are "capsule offices" furnished with chairs, desks, and message boards that convert into beds. Western entrepreneurs have been dreaming up other applications, such as capsule lodgings for prisons, airports, college dorms, and ski resorts.

Capsule accommodations such as Tokyo's Cockpit Hotel or Business Pillow Inn at the very least discourage sleepwalking. Should you ever find yourself inside a capsule hotel bed tucked in a little bit too snugly, there's only one sure way to fight the insomnia brought on by claustrophobia: lie back, relax . . . and start counting itsy-bitsy, teeny-tiny sheep.

Safe Sex and Quaint, Too

RABU HOTERU

love hotel

Ever dreamt of a romantic fling in a turreted castle or in an alien spaceship? In Japan, such dreams come true at "love hotels," special establishments designed expressly for the amorous encounter. Beckoning with names such as Hotel Casanova, Hotel Passion, Hotel Utopia, and Hotel Once More—usually proclaimed in glowing neon—love hotels are fashioned after pleasure boats, pyramids, and even the London Bridge. The ship *Queen Mary* has been sighted outside Tokyo, moored alongside a highway. The Statue of Liberty, too.

Like eccentric, X-rated theme parks, an estimated thirty-five thousand love hotels cluster along major thoroughfares and in cities nationwide. Inside, high-tech toys add to that certain *je ne sais quoi*. In many such hotels, control panels let patrons adjust  rotating beds and laser disc *karaoke* (sing-along machines), while soft-porn images flicker in the background. One sports-theme hotel lets fans fulfill fantasies in motorized racing-car beds. For those willing to take a chance with love, a gambling theme hotel is equipped with slot machines and a rotating bed in the shape of a roulette wheel. In one establishment, toboggans run from the bath to the mattress. And another hotel offers musical waterbeds and glass-bottomed bathtubs on pedestals. Magnifying glass, that is.

Despite the gaudy gizmos, love hotels actually provide a simple, down-home commodity: privacy. A couple discreetly drives into the hotel, parks in a one-car garage (the door automatically closes to conceal the license plate), and slips in and out of a room without once looking a stranger in the eye. To limit awkward chance encounters, one elevator escorts guests up to their rooms while another ushers them out. In lieu of a concierge, computerized consoles display a menu of possible hotel room interiors. After selecting the fantasy room of their choice, couples follow an illuminated arrow to the appropriate place. A time-clock at check-in keeps track of the length of the stay and electric sensors inside the rooms monitor the use or purchase of accessories. Guests can stay for a short "rest" or a full night's "stay," and when it comes time to settle the bill, they simply pay an anonymous hand through a slot at the checkout counter.

All this privacy is not only ideal for illicit affairs but is also convenient for married couples, who comprise a healthy percentage of all weekend guests. Crowded together at home with extended families in rooms separated by paper-thin walls, if not screens, couples find that it's not easy to feel sexy with a mother-in-law on the other side of the partition. And apparently Japanese grandparents chafe for a bit of privacy, too.

A growing number of love hotel guests are the over-sixty set who take advantage of the economical morning to early-evening rates. Because of their popularity, love hotels have become hot properties for investors. The hotels turn a profit by charging hourly rates for rooms used an average of three times a day. Precise earnings elude verification, however, since even the most energetic tax official couldn't possibly keep track of the number of guests who come and go.

Not everyone has a passion for love hotels. In an attempt to throw cold water on the industry, the upright officials of one city tried to outlaw double beds in hotels located in "respectable" areas. Likewise, many have voiced a preference for more tasteful love hotels, a seeming contradiction in terms. Bowing to these pressures, some new establishments have become determined to clean up their images and have replaced vulgar masonry and titillating devices with sing-along machines, suntanning parlors, jet baths, and saunas. Moreover, a number of hotels have adopted the European custom of placing a little wrapped gift on each guest's pillow at night—except that instead of chocolates, they leave condoms. It's safe sex and quaint, too!

Despite their critics, the pyramids and castles continue to line the highways. And the pleasure boats do not seem likely to weigh anchor anytime soon.

Cupid Works in Mysterious Ways

SEKKUSU

sex

___

Sex just doesn't make sense in Japan. Saying "I love you" to your sweetie in public is out. Openly enjoying sexually explicit comic books is in. Flaunting photos of nudes showing pubic hair is out. Enjoying coed nude bathing is in. Disrobing in the locker room without first swathing yourself in a towel is out. Chatting matter-of-factly about sex is in. Go figure.

Traditional Japanese couples tend to express their affection privately. For instance, rather than walking hand-in-hand or cooing over each other, they might show their closeness simply by addressing each other with the intimate form of "you." Moreover, the Japanese have their share of sexual inhibitions. Nudity in film or print is acceptable only if the naughty bits are first scratched out by censors. Homosexuality is so taboo that, except in very circumscribed areas, it hardly exists in Japan—or so people say. Japanese women, lacking a serious feminist movement, are often depicted as mere sexual objects in the mass media. And in close-knit

Japanese society, media reporting on extra-marital affairs can easily lead to shame and scandal, as in the case of the occasional sumo wrestling champion or politician who falls from public grace when caught with his proverbial pants down.

Paradoxically, inhabitants of this land of the famous erotic woodblock print can also be quite uninhibited when it comes to sex. For instance, it's not uncommon for unmarried couples in their twenties to celebrate Christmas Eve by openly renting expensive hotel rooms and making love. Similarly, love hotels are considered part of life, and frank television shows about, say, breast size are unlikely to cause widespread blushing. Moreover, until 1958, licensed prostitutes were free to ply their trade in districts such as Yoshiwara. (A Japanese hooker, incidentally, should not be confused with the geisha, who is a lady skilled in the art of entertaining.)

Japan has its share of lurid striptease joints (which encourage on-stage customer participation) and sex tours to Southeast Asia. There's even a street of brothels in Bangkok set aside strictly for the Japanese. Prostitution is also rampant locally at the Japanese bathhouses called "soaplands"—which used to be named Turkish baths until the Turks objected.

In Japan, as everywhere else perhaps, there's no clear line between love and lust, and ultimately it may be futile to try to make sense of any of it. Suffice it to say that whether or not you happen to be Japanese, Cupid works in mysterious ways.

Lame Ducks in Love

DOKUSHIN

bachelor

Twenty Japanese *dokushin*, or bachelors, became so exasperated with the single life and their inability to find spouses in their remote hometown prefecture of Akita that they reportedly drove their tractors all the way to Tokyo and brandished signs reading: "Bride, Come To Me! Come To Akita!"

As this escapade suggests, unmarried Japanese men, particularly those in rural areas, are becoming increasingly frustrated in their search for that certain special someone in Japan. Some claim that the introduction of women's lib to Japan and the surplus of available males have caused eligible Japanese women to become more choosy in their choice of husbands. Whatever the reason, this *oyome-san mondai*, or "bride problem," has left a growing number of bachelors worried that they will simply not be marriage material unless they can woo prospective wives with *sankoo*, meaning "the top three" qualifications for marriage: top resume, top income, and top height.

A man who fails to marry by age thirty-one risks being dismissed as a *toshikoshi soba*, a reference to the noodle eaten on the thirty-first day of December—the last day of the year. The flip side of this less-than-flattering food metaphor is "Christmas cake," meaning a Japanese woman who fails to wed by age twenty-five. Like a Christmas cake which remains uneaten after the twenty-fifth of December, a lady who remains unwed past age twenty-five is said to risk becoming stale and undesirable. Ignoring such warnings, many of today's Japanese women increasingly prefer to postpone marriage and wait until their thirties to tie the knot. To some such singles, a career and financial independence are simply more inviting than the prospect of living with a spouse in cramped quarters. And babies and live-in in-laws make six.

In an effort to increase their odds of finding a wife, some desperate bachelors have resorted to *hanamuko gakkoo*, or classes geared to enhancing marriage prospects. At institutions such as Marriage Man Academy, a would-be groom learns in six short months such necessities as how to understand a woman's feelings, how to tell jokes to the opposite sex, and how best to part his hair.

The predicament of Japanese bachelors has also spawned a thriving industry for professionals who specialize in *omiai*, or arranged marriages. In one version of the traditional omiai—still going strong today—a *nakoodo*, or go-between, sets up an initial meeting between a prospective pair and then removes herself from the scene. In another modern-day version of omiai, corporate cupids with names such as Nippon Bridal Bank provide computer dating services, handpicked mate-matching, and a monthly magazine of potential partners (photos included, of course). Such businesses have also established foreign subsidiaries to cater to Japanese lonely hearts living abroad. A typical fee might be eight percent of a bachelor's annual salary in the event the service leads to wedding bells. For Japanese bachelors who are perennially lame ducks in love, still another option is importing one's betrothed from abroad. In what have been termed "instant marriages," a Japanese man can hire an international marriage broker who will direct him to a foreign country to choose a bride from a group of prescreened candidates.

In Japan, where even the heir to the throne was once chided for his difficulty in finding a wife, eligible "bachelorettes" may often seem to feel less pressure than men about whom and when to wed. Basking in this new-found freedom, some single women describe their ideal marriage as *ie tsuki, kuruma tsuki, baba nuki*—"I want a house and a car, but not a mother-in-law living at home."

"Have a Nice Blendship"

KISSATEN

coffee shop

Anyone who has ever set foot in a *kissaten*, or Japanese coffee shop, can confirm that the land of ancient tea ceremonies is actually a modern-day coffee-drinker's paradise.

Ease yourself into the cushy chair of a cozy kissaten (*kissa* for short) and forget the troubles of the day. The waiter materializes in a flash. Bowing solemnly, he or she instantly produces ice water, a refreshing damp towel (hot in the winter, cold in the summer), and a lengthy list of *burendo* (blends of coffee). The choice typically ranges from Vienna Roast to Mandarin to Kilimanjaro to Blue Mountain to Guatemalan to Colombian, and much, much more. Some kissaten are outfitted with coils, burners, glass bulbs, measuring spoons, and flat wooden stirrers better suited to a chemist's laboratory than to a coffee shop, and customers may specify the precise bean/water ratio or brewing temperature. Fans of ice coffee (*aisu koohii*) will rejoice when they find that sugar is served in the form of

syrup so as to dissolve evenly in the cup. And customers with a sweet tooth can indulge in coffee jelly (topped with whipped cream if they wish). In short, Japanese coffee never fails to please as long as one steers clear of so-called American coffee—ample and weak, and tasting faintly of soap suds.

Japanese coffee cups are dainty, thimble-sized vessels resembling receptacles for some rare elixir. In certain establishments, the aesthetically attuned customer may select the pattern of china most compatible with the desired brand of coffee. The cup is then lovingly positioned with the handle on the left so that the right hand is free for stirring. (Left-handed drinkers can opt for tea.)

Each kissaten enjoys a character all its own. Comic book kissa are stacked with reams of comic books, pumped with rock music, and generously supplied with video games. English-language kissa allow students to brush up on conversation skills. And business kissa are fully outfitted with word processors, copiers, and—what else in Japan—fax machines. Jazz kissa offer warm lighting and soft jazz. Music fans might also try "Jive Coffee," now available in cans. The can's label explains: "The origin of the word 'jive' came from playing or dancing to jazz."

For coffee-drinkers on the fringe there was a fad for the *no-pan kissa* (no panties kissa) offering a tasteless combination of coffee, panty-less waitresses, and mirrored floors. And for high net-worth caffeine connoisseurs, there is at least one ultra-elite café. For a few hundred dollars per cup, guests at this establishment sit in splendor beneath French Impressionist paintings, sip gold-dusted coffee brewed with imported water, and try their best to look nonchalant and famous. Another favorite is the French-styled kissaten, such as Café Fifi, Déjà Vu, or Le Gâteau. There, even pastries that look classically French are usually filled with local fare such as red beans and Japanese pumpkin. These mock-continental cafés evoke an old-world charm through fleur-de-lis wallpaper and red velvet chairs.

Known originally as undistinguished *miruku hooru* (milk halls), kissaten flourished in Japan in the 1950s as the place to savor coffee, a fashionable Western delicacy. Unlike green tea, which is usually doled out gratis, coffee in Japan is considered a mark of sophistication, and customers are charged accordingly. Today, kissaten have become such an institution that meeting in front of the pink-and-white-striped awning of the Almond Confectionery and Coffee Shop at the intersection of Tokyo's bustling Roppongi district is akin to a rendezvous for cheese-cake at Lindy's near Manhattan's Rockefeller Center, and the phrase "Shall we go for coffee?" has become the standard Japanese pickup line. In recent years, however, the escalation of land prices has milked the profits of many kissaten and the number of coffee shops has decreased as a result. This trend has paved the way for stand-up, self-service kissa—ideal for the hyperactive salaryman or office lady on the run who needs to refuel in a jiff. One such chain, Doutor, promotes its fresh-roasted, blended coffee with the perky pitch, "Have a nice blendship."

When tourists balk at a four-dollar cup of coffee, they forget that Japanese coffee is truly the cream of the cream. In fact, the discerning connoisseur can raise only one real objection to the Japanese kissaten: no free refills.

A Retailer's Vision of Oz

DEPAATO

department store

Even in the face of stiffer competition from large discount retail chains, the Japanese depaato, or department store, is, by Western standards, still a retailer's vision of Oz. Like a tiny glistening city, each depaato overflows with smiling attendants, jewel-like shops, and sumptuously wrapped goods. In stressful Japan, the depaato is also a thoroughly therapeutic refuge for those who need some place to escape. When the going gets tough, the Japanese go shopping.

Most Japanese department stores are prestigious establishments that go beyond selling mere lamps and lingerie. Originally called *hyakkaten*, or "stores of one hundred items," they provide a full day's entertainment for the whole family, offering art exhibits, films, concerts, sports clubs, roof gardens, shrines, travel centers, restaurants, and toddlers' play areas. Traditionalists can find that perfect silk kimono or bonsai tree, while name-conscious consumers can cruise for labels such as Bill Blass or Tiffany.

Service is stellar, too. After graduating from rigorous training programs, many depaato attendants start their mornings inspired by their supervisors' pep talks on how best to court the customer. They then assemble on the front lines behind sales counters or roam the halls in search of game. Information-desk clerks dressed like Barbie dolls in pillbox caps and white gloves direct the public with a flourish of the hand and a ceremonious closing bow. Perfumed elevator operators, bedecked in hats and gloves, shuttle up and down in polished brass lifts and deliver falsetto-voiced speeches about each floor's treasures. Since the elevators are automatic, the operators seem superfluous, but they are actually an all-important sign that the customer is supreme.

To help the indecisive shopper select the perfect present, some depaato provide "gift consultation centers." And while many harried Western sales clerks shun gift-wrapping as an unnecessary frill, the depaato personnel still bind, box, and wrap just about anything in sight. Clerks will lovingly treat the smallest package of rice crackers like an exquisite offering, providing multilayered paper, elaborate ribbons, and bags within bags within bags. Then, on request, they will cheerfully ship the paltry purchase to the other side of the globe.

For those partial to gastronomic pampering, the secret weapon of most depaato is the well-appointed food section, usually tucked away on the lower level. There, sales personnel hawk the store's wares by plying customers with free tastes of delicacies ranging from Japanese soybean (available in paste or soup), to imported French wines, to—what seems like nirvana for the starved Western tourist—thick slices of imported U.S.

steak. Salesmen spoon-feed these samples to the happy shoppers while force-feeding them a hard-sell speech on the goods. To discourage greedy customers from dining out daily on the free offerings in the food department, some stores quietly remove their choicest samples during the lunch and dinner hours. There's also an unspoken rule limiting each patron to just one taste—breach this and you're liable to find a livid attendant springing out from behind the counter and shouting (in flawless English, if necessary): "One . . . piece . . . ONLY!"

Even with the bursting of Japan's economic bubble, the depaato is still a dazzling display of conspicuous consumption that caters to affluent consumers who are willing to pay a premium in such elite stores as Mitsukoshi or Seibu. (The latter has so much clout that it even once signed on the reclusive Woody Allen to promote it.) And for the increasingly yen-conscious customer, Japan's no-frills department stores still provide cordial clerks and bargains galore.

In terms of service, selection, and display, the depaato comes close to perfecting the Western prototype, even when it occasionally misses the mark in interpreting foreign motifs. One yuletide season, an overly eager Tokyo depaato unveiled a window display featuring a robust Santa Claus. The only problem . . . he was fastened to a cross.

If a Coke Machine Calls Out in the Forest. . . .

JIDOOHANBAIKI

vending machine

In a deserted forest somewhere in rural Japan, a chirpy voice calls out to no one: "Would you like orange juice or Coke?" The speaker is one of Japan's ubiquitous *jidoohanbaiki*, or vending machines, which nowadays literally litter the landscape and have finally learned to talk.

Although old-fashioned vending machines were content to sell their wares silently, today's Japanese machines apparently prefer a more vocal approach. One chatty tea-vending machine equipped with a microcomputer reportedly informs astonished consumers, "I'm a vending robot, a tea sales girl. . . . Let's chat." Another model flirtatiously blinks and beeps at customers and then reminds them, "Please do not forget your change . . . and dispose of your cup properly." Still another soft-drink machine in search of conversation has a built-in microphone for the customer to respond orally when the machine asks if ice cubes are desired.

The world leader in automated everything, Japan provides one vending machine for every ten people—the world's highest per capita rate. Mere soda machines or candy dispensers are child's play for the versatile Japanese vending machine industry, which has dreamt up automated dispensers to sell items such as diapers, dried squid, Bibles, socks, soup, Shinto shrine oracles, boiled eggs, roses, condoms, fresh vegetables, chopsticks, floppy disks, imported U.S. beef, and, of course, Coke. Since vending machine vandalism is virtually nonexistent in relatively crime-free Japan, some Japanese machines even sell jewels such as amethysts and strings of genuine pearls. There are also match-making machines that dispense romance in plastic capsules. In the ultimate twentieth-century blind date, the female consumer opens the capsule to find a slip of paper revealing her potential partner's picture, name, number, horoscope, and (a crucial component) the type of car he drives. Not to worry, all "dates" are prescreened for prestigious university and company affiliations before their bios are placed in the capsules.

Vice is also mechanically vended in Japan. So-called white machines discreetly dispense white panties bearing suggestive sayings while other naughty machines sell whiskey, cigarettes, and pornographic magazines. Although popular among self-conscious consumers who prefer to make certain purchases in private, these machines have been attacked by groups such as the Council on Intruding Vending Machines, which argue that instant access to vice only leads to juvenile delinquency. Taking such criticism to heart, certain vendors have designed machines which cover up the sex magazines during daylight hours and shine forth in all their swank and glory at night.

Like a tribute to the nation's reputation for excellent service, the Japanese vending machine politely dishes out service without once wincing or taking a break. One train station ticket machine, for example, displays a cartoon image of a female train conductor smartly outfitted in tie and cap. The figure greets the customer by blinking WELCOME and says goodbye by bowing and flashing: THANK YOU VERY MUCH.

Some Japanese vending machines also dispense their fair share of frustration, whether by returning the incorrect change or by disgorging green tea even when the button clearly says "café au lait." At such times, the irate consumer can try kicking or shaking the metal beast, but chances are that such efforts will come to naught. And to add insult to injury, as the offended customer storms away in a huff, a cheeky electronic voice behind him or her may sing, *"Arigatoo gozaimashita! Arigatoo gozaimashita!"*—"Thank you very much! Thank you very much!"

And so, through the jidoohanbaiki, the Japanese have succeeded in adding yet another dimension to that age-old question: If a Coke machine calls out in the forest, and nobody hears its cries. . . ?

Gastronomic Good Looks

SHOKUHIN SAMPURU

sample food

I n the Kappabashi ("Bridge of the Water Imp") area of Tokyo, a frosty mug of beer stands frozen in time, like a commercial on pause. Next to it, a piece of two-week-old sushi sits stoically on the shelf, and a pair of chopsticks hovers over a bowl of ramen, suspended in midair by a single strand of noodle. Customers eagerly queue up to order these dubious delicacies, but no one dares to eat them.

There's a simple explanation for this creepy culinary condition. Kappabashi is Japan's restaurant supply district, where the "food" is actually *shokuhin sampuru* (food samples) composed entirely of plastic. Japanese restaurateurs buy the samples of fake food and then display them prominently in their windows to advertise the real selections inside. The idea is that, in Japan, gastronomic good looks can be as tempting as taste.

Japan's visual menus date back to the 1920s, when sample food was first used to reassure cautious customers about dining on foreign fare. Those first samples, real food coated with wax, were eventually replaced by models made entirely of wax. Today, plastic has replaced wax in a food sample industry that generates hundreds of millions of dollars in annual sales.

Learning to whip up plastic food takes years of painstaking practice. The apprentice begins with basic buckwheat noodles (*soba*), graduates to sushi and fish scales, and finally, one day, proudly launches his or her first lobster. Skillful technique is appreciated not only by masters of the trade, but also by non-Japanese speaking customers who gesture frantically at these realistic models when attempting to order dinner.

Westerners are gradually growing hungry for sample food and Japanese producers are all too happy to cater. Although American restaurants still show little appetite for the products, U.S. amusement parks, art galleries, and gift shops are eating up these cooked-up imports. In fact, many Westerners now feast on asparagus pens, corn-on-the-cob erasers, chocolate-chip key chains, and sushi clocks. And at bedtime, some even snore in the soothing soporific glow of fried-egg night lights, comforted by the thought that their valuables are safely concealed inside imitation heads of lettuce. The hollow, plastic "Lett-us-hide" looks exactly like an iceberg lettuce and would fool any intruder who neglected to scrutinize the vegetables in the fridge.

Food samples may cause some stomachs to growl while making others want to skip lunch altogether, but then *chacun à son goût*. Transfixed by a plastic spaghetti that snakes up from its plate to a floating fork, the diner recalls the deliciously haunting images of Salvador Dali. Perhaps food samples should ideally be situated in one of his landscapes, suspended in a surreal twilight where reality blurs with illusion and things never rot.

A Toilet Smarter Than Its User

TOIRE

toilet

Ask for the bathroom in Japan and you'll be directed to a room with a bathtub and nothing more. Ask for the toilet *(toire)*, and you may find yourself awash in unexpected possibilities.

Japanese lavatories are either Western-style (the sit-down variety) or Japanese—an elongated bowl flanked by foot pads. To use the Japanese-style loo, don special plastic "toilet slippers," position feet as directed, squat, and let nature do the rest. (Unless you have a sumo wrestler's sense of balance, you'll find that these johns cut down drastically on bathroom reading.) Even a Western-style toilet can turn out to be a surprising adventure now that Japan is undergoing a "toilet boom," meaning a demand for the latest in Western-style bathroom technology. In the past, toilets were a taboo subject, but today newfangled toiletry has somehow managed to capture the Japanese imagination and flood the market.

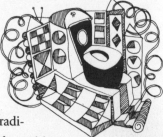

Picture yourself entering a traditional tatami-mat Japanese abode, retiring to the powder room, and suddenly confronting a complex computerized commode that looks as if it requires a pilot's license to operate. After a few moments on the preheated, self-washing, comfort-controlled toilet seat, the unwary may reach for toilet paper, only to find a panel of buttons instead. Push one and an oscillating nozzle under the bowl's rim subjects your unsuspecting underside to a wash-and-blow-dry jet-stream treatment that includes spray deodorant. Welcome, dear friends, to the world of the "shower toilet."

In the best Japanese households, the shower toilet may soon be replaced by an even newer model, the Washlet Queen. Just punch one button on the hand-held remote control and it analyzes body temperature, blood pressure, and weight. Finally, what the world has been waiting for: a toilet smarter than its user.

With the introduction of high-tech toiletry, the whole family can now get into the act. For the demure housewife who flushes an average of 2.5 times per use to camouflage unseemly bathroom noises but who nonetheless wants to conserve water, there is the Etiquettone or Sound Princess—a cassette which simulates the sound of flushing water. For the more music-minded, there's a toilet paper roll that plays Beethoven when the paper is pulled. And for the absent-minded husband who routinely forgets to lower the seat after use, there's the Beep Seat, which goes off sixty seconds after the seat has been raised. Even kitty can now revel in a state-of-the-art litter box: equipped with infrared detectors and cat-hair filters, it flushes automatically after each use.

As if domestic bathroom bliss were not enough, a

movement to clean up Japan's public johns is being spearheaded by the JTA, or Japanese Toilet Association. Comprised in part of architects, doctors, and plumbers, the JTA was described by one Japanese news service as "a voluntary network of individuals and information entirely dedicated to the toilet." The JTA has sponsored an international toilet symposium, sent delegations abroad to advise on foreign facilities, and even established Good Toilet Day (it's November 10, for those who wish to mark their calendars). Thanks to the JTA, there is also now a *Toilet News Bulletin*, a permanent Toilet Expo (complete with demonstration rooms), and, on Shikoku Island, a two-story suite of lavatories known as the Charm Station. Come to the Charm Station and experience restrooms in the style of fin de siècle Vienna and Louis XIV—thrones literally fit for a king.

What can the next step be in Japan's efforts to refine the toilet? According to a representative of the Japan Toilet Association, experts are already hard at work on a proposal for people to have toilets installed . . . in their cars.

Japan's Leading Indoor Sport

PACHINKO

pinball

Row after row of participants sit immersed in deep concentration, focusing all energy on a point in front of them. The setting is not the solemn chambers of an ancient Buddhist temple, but rather a pinball arcade where the Japanese play one of their favorite games. It's called *pachinko*.

The pachinko parlor is the home away from home for housewives, businessmen, teenagers, grandmothers, and other pachinko addicts. The object of the vertical pinball game (officially viewed as a game of skill since most forms of gambling are illegal in Japan) is to shoot miniature steel balls through a maze of steel pins into holes in order to win more balls. The balls are then exchanged for small prizes, such as candy, toothpaste, and socks, which, in turn, can be exchanged for tax-free cash outside the parlor in black-market buy-back booths.

The exteriors of pachinko arcades are an explosion of gaudy, pulsating neon rivaling Manhattan's cheesy Times Square. A poster outside one popular arcade depicts a gangster pulling the trigger of a gun and shouting, "Big Chance! . . . BAM! BAM!" Inside parlors such as the Gold Mine, blinding fluorescent lights illuminate billowing clouds of cigarette smoke as rows of mesmerized players sit alone in front of glass-encased machines, transfixed by the crashing of metal balls against glass in an onomatopoeic "pachinko! pachinko! pachinko!" (the sound that gave the game its name). Bells, blaring music, and exhortations broadcast over loudspeakers egg on customers at an ear-splitting decibel level that would make even rap singers beg for mercy. At the exits of the parlors, a sink with soap is available for players who want to wash their hands of the whole experience.

True pachinko fans find the atmosphere thrilling, the crash of metal balls cathartic, and the money eminently enticing (a few hundred yen's worth of winnings can quickly multiply). And for those serious about the game, special television shows offer instruction in pachinko, and pachinko academies such as the venerable Institute of Pachinko Technology can, with a little bit of elbow grease, turn the armchair arcade amateur into a polished "pachi-pro." Such schools continue to insist that pachinko is a game of skill despite the introduction of new automated microchip machines that make the winnings more random and thus threaten to sideline the pros permanently.

While pachinko operators rack up huge profits in what is still Japan's leading indoor sport, a few also maintain an unsportsmanlike reputation for flagrant tax evasion. When the Japanese tax office attempted to monitor pachinko industry income and tax liability through the use of prepaid, electronic pachinko cards, some operators protested vehemently and reportedly donated over one million dollars to "tilt" the opinion of powerful politicians. In the ensuing scandal—aptly termed "Pachinko-gate"—allegations ricocheted like metal balls, and a number of politicians risked abruptly finding their political game . . . over.

Genuinely Teed Off

GORUFU KICHIGAI

"golf crazy"

In a country where open space is at a premium, the desire to master golf may seem slightly nutty, but then the Japanese are, after all, nuts about golf.

In Tokyo, playing a round on even the plainest of public courses costs over $150. Some brokerage firms deal exclusively in the precious commodity of golf memberships, and the most desirable golf clubs charge million-dollar membership fees. Reserving a tee-off time on courses can take months, and even driving ranges (which are often a three- or four-hour drive away) tend to require reservations. Once on a green, players are encouraged to keep the ball rolling; in fact, on some crowded courses a control tower ensures that golfers tee off every seven minutes.

Because of the dearth and expense of Japanese golf courses, only a small percentage of golfers regularly get to play on real greens. The rest settle for such innovative compromises as a driving range nestled on top of a building; a full-scale, glass-encased sand trap in the sports area of a department store; or a ball tethered to a tee in a neighborhood alley. One determined soul reportedly set about polishing his swing on a subway station platform, only to be sued by an injured commuter who was genuinely teed off.

Another way to economize on golf in Japan is to travel abroad to play the sport—often a bargain, even figuring airfare and hotel costs. Still another option is the amazing "golf simulator." Players select their favorite golf course from around the world, step in front of an image of it projected onto a large canvas, and, using a real club and ball, whack away to their heart's content. The simulator calculates the ball's trajectory, tracks the shot on a video monitor, and even offers helpful tips on the golfer's swing. A more modest version of the simulator is the "Handy 01." After a player swings a club over this computer's "Science Eye" sensor, the device calculates the distance and speed of the shot.

For executives with an eye to client development, almost nothing beats an invitation to partake in eighteen holes on luscious links followed by a hot soak in the club's communal bath. Junior executives who don't play shouldn't count on hobnobbing with key clients anytime soon, and experienced players should keep their handicap in check since the boss might not take kindly to losing too often. Outside of work, too, golf has enormous appeal in Japan, maybe because even the most overcrowded course seems to offer a peaceful respite from a frenetic Japanese metropolis. Perhaps capitalizing on this sentiment, Japan's Church of Perfect Liberty, nicknamed the Golf Church, reportedly preaches that golf is one path to spiritual development.

With the Japanese putting so much energy into putting, the

ultimate satisfaction must be a hole-in-one, right? Wrong. As in some other countries, the golfer who lands this ace shot is obligated to celebrate the blessed event by tipping the caddie generously, treating club members to drinks, and maybe even throwing a party. To cover these exorbitant costs, some enterprising Japanese companies now actually sell "hole-in-one insurance."

You don't have to be crazy about golf to play in Japan. Just crazy.

Look out, Mickey Mouse

MANGA

comic books

The samurai wheels around, his sword flashes, and a scarlet fountain erupts in its wake. . . . Elsewhere, the drooling villain finally puts his victim out of her misery after lurid torture that would shock even the Marquis de Sade.

Outsiders marvel at Japan's orderly society, yet the world of *manga*, or Japanese comics, rages with graphic violence and perversion. Today, reveling in the private pleasures of manga has become so widespread that an estimated one billion of these comic books are purchased each year.

Although the word *"manga"* was coined in the early nineteenth century, Japan's comic book craze took off only in the 1960s. It was then that publishers first came up with the marketing brain wave of targeting the postpubescent set. Today, many Japanese cartoons are themselves, in a sense, "grown up": unlike American comics, they often include long, involved stories and relatively realistic drawings.

The comic book format has proved so versatile in Japan

that manga are now read by kids, grandparents, stock boys, office ladies, and CEOs. If you want to reach Japanese readers, manga is the medium, and the message spans a multitude of topics. Even the most unlikely nonfiction subjects are addressed in cartoon form. For example, there's a manga on foreign aid published by the Japanese Foreign Ministry; a manga on the workings of the Tokyo Stock Exchange; a manga handbook for employees of a major steel company; and even a comic book guide to the legal profession.

Manga is a fast medium, providing instant entertainment to folks with little time to spare. At the same time, these comics can offer a revealing insight into what some Japanese are really thinking. For instance, during the Persian Gulf War crisis, the popular *Silent Service* manga reflected Japanese frustration at being forced to pick up the tab for what some perceived as a war-mongering United States. *Silent Service* features the idealistic captain of a Japanese nuclear submarine who is under the command of the U.S. fleet. Unable to accept subservience to the Americans, the feisty Japanese skipper becomes a renegade who eventually prompts the Americans to aim missiles at Tokyo and Osaka.

Most startling is the graphic (and often violent) sex depicted in many manga. Open a random Japanese comic book and you may read about buxom uniformed schoolgirls falling prey to a lecherous attacker. Next time you ride on a Japanese subway, peer over your neighbor's shoulder. Don't be surprised if he or she is unabashedly reading *Enema Rock Climbing* or even *Rape Man*, in which the protagonist commits rape after rape.

Pressured by groups such as the Japanese Association to

Protect Children from Comics, publishers are now starting to put "Adult Comic" stickers on some manga, and store owners are similarly being advised to keep sex manga away from minors. Nonetheless, sexually explicit comics are still available in convenience stores and even streetside vending machines across the country. While Japanese censors have strictly curbed non-comic-book porn, they apparently have a special place in their hearts for manga of all kinds.

At an average newsstand price of a few dollars per copy, and with a massive circulation, Japanese comics have become so lucrative that their publishers are beginning to export them. Americans can also now subscribe to *Mangajin*, a magazine of Japanese cartoons translated into English and published throughout the year. Skeptics may question whether Westerners will ever acquire a taste for Japanese-style manga, but manga fans insist that an immense English-language manga market is not far away. So watch out, Superheroes: *Enema Rock Climbing* may be just around the corner.

A Ride as Smooth as Tofu

SHINKANSEN

bullet train

"Faster than a speeding bullet . . . ?" Well, not quite, but Japan's *shinkansen*, or super-express bullet train, is fast, safe, punctual, and comfortable—a real dream of a locomotive. For long-distance travel, the bullet is the only way to go. Inside the gleaming, green-and-white shinkansen (the world's first high-speed train), travelers happily snooze through their journeys as the landscape flashes by the windows and the speedometer merrily climbs to a cruising speed of 130 miles per hour.

Established in 1964, just in time for the Tokyo Olympics, the shinkansen played a key role in Japan's economic success by linking major cities. Today, the bullet reduces the former six-and-a-half-hour train trip between Tokyo and Osaka to just a heartbeat under three hours. The train is so punctual that passengers have barely one minute to disembark. The shinkansen waits for no man. The bullet also has a sterling safety record, in part because its central computer system

stops the train automatically at the slightest indication of earth-quake, faulty signal, or other emergency. Aboard the bullet, one quickly forgets the hassles of conventional train travel since the windows are soundproof and the ride is as smooth as tofu.

Passengers who become peckish but who forgot to pack a lunch are in good hands on the shinkansen. At regular inter-vals, a smartly dressed hostess miraculously appears at the door of the compartment, bows to the assembled, and announces, "I'm sorry to disturb you" (a ritual she repeats when leaving). She then produces a trolley piled high with boxed lunches, beverages (including an ingeniously designed canister for steeping green tea), snacks, and souvenirs—in short, an enticing assortment of impeccably wrapped goodies that puts to shame the wounded fruit pastries available on America's Amtrak trains. For travelers who pass up these offer-ings, a buffet car serves an appetizing selection of Japanese and Western dishes.

For those who can't get enough of a good thing, the bullet train's first-class cars, called Green Cars, are available at a pre-mium. Telephones are located throughout the train, and there are separate compartments for wash basins, Japanese-style or Western-style toilets, and urinals. The latter is not for the bash-ful since a small glass window placed at the top of the urinal door reveals (somewhat unnecessarily, one feels) the identity of the user.

The shinkansen is not exactly cheap. But as skyrocketing housing costs push Japanese further away from their work-places, companies are starting to pay for employees to commute daily on the bullet train. In addition, foreigners with tourist visas can purchase an economical shinkansen pass that affords unlimited train travel and makes trekking through Japan literally a breeze.

Sardines Never Had It This Good

CHIKATETSU

subway

While the elite cover huge distances ensconced in Japan's bullet trains, mere mortals routinely travel shorter stretches on a more pedestrian mode of transport: the *chikatetsu*, or subway. Tokyo's chikatetsu have become so crowded during the peak hours that they are now an exercise in commuter claustrophobia, or what the Japanese call *tsuukin-jigoku*, meaning "commuter hell." Inside the trains, routinely packed to almost three times recommended capacity, bodies are so compressed that some of the newest subway cars have virtually done away with seats altogether. There's no need to hang onto the subway straps since the surrounding mob will prop you up like a neatly stacked domino.

During the morning rush hour, the world-renowned white-gloved "pushers," determined to keep the wheels of Japanese productivity rolling, cram stray limbs of passengers into the subway cars. Worse still, crowded trains often include the dreaded *chikan*,

or subway molester, who lets his hands wander freely. In an effort to ease the burden on commuters, some companies are introducing flexible working hours that let employees avoid the commuter crush. While most Japanese seem resigned to the misery of subway overcrowding, one group of feisty older ladies has started to fight back. Nicknamed the "obatallions"— a combination of the Japanese words for "older women" and "aliens"—these determined women use their sharp elbows and pointy umbrellas as weapons to create space for themselves on board.

At hours when there is more room to breathe, Japanese subways become surprisingly pleasant. They are spotless (graffiti is unheard of in Japan) and reliable according to posted schedules, and Tokyo station stops are conveniently color-coded and labeled in both Japanese and English. Subway platforms are marked with raised paths to guide the blind, the seats are plush and velvety, and special Silver Seats are reserved for the elderly and infirm. Subway theft, while recently somewhat on the rise, is still so rare that passengers routinely leave their bags unattended in the overhead racks (only stray umbrellas are fair game for thieves). Ticket-takers in some stations greet the morning commuters with a rousing chorus of "Good morning!" Even more impressive, each time a train pulls out, a white-gloved attendant marks the departure by deftly performing a graceful dip and spin of the hand—a semi-acrobatic gesture worthy of figure skating's famous "flying camels."

From the sublime to the not-so-sublime, Japanese bullet trains and subways are the products of a nation that has raised train travel to an art. For short-distance trips, the amenities of Japanese subways almost compensate for the lack of oxygen. Sardines never had it this good.

A Standing-Room-Only Experience

KOMU

crowded

Like an aquatic rock concert, Japanese public pools are a standing-room-only experience: the water brims with a sea of swimmers searching frantically for a free place to paddle. In a country as *komu* (crowded) as Japan, inhabitants feel the constant urge to escape the waves of people and try to come up for air.

Well over one hundred million Japanese are shoe-horned into a nation the size of Montana, and only a third of it is inhabitable. Tokyo, Japan's most populated city, is so crammed that some advocate creating a new capital to alleviate the congestion. City dwellers are packed into so-called rabbit-hutch housing that leaves precious little room for dinner parties, children's recreation, or even romantic interludes.

Because of the lack of space, staircases are kept narrow and steep, which is fine if you happen to be an amateur rock-climber. Toilets such as the "Slim-U" (short for "slim urinal") are squeezed into Lilliputian corners. Some bicycles have extra-narrow handlebars to help reduce sideswiping on narrow city sidewalks. Pedestrians in teaming train stations obediently squeeze to the left to avoid the commuter crush. On overrun ski areas, charting a non-collision downhill course has become a sport of its own. Even cemeteries are becoming so packed that authorities are considering alternatives to traditional plots. Cramped conditions also mean that unwanted sounds are always around the corner. To silence noisy dogs, some reportedly resort to anti-bark shock collars.

In desperate attempts to flee the hordes, some Japanese dive into their cars and drive in search of peace and privacy. Yet, grinding through gridlock in bumper-to-bumper traffic is a dubious cure for claustrophobia. To make matters worse, parking lots are so limited that drivers park in space-saving car elevators that stack up automobiles neatly in tiers, like cozy bunkbeds. Car owners can't even register their vehicles until they can prove they have places to park. As a result, owners of so-called homeless cars (meaning cars without parking spots) now sometimes turn to car dealers and manufacturers for assistance in locating the precious spaces.

Finding a little breathing room is a constant challenge in this condensed country. No wonder that some Japanese got a little testy a few years back when they heard the government's suggested solution to the nation's declining birthrate: offer incentives for families to have more kids.

And a Video to Show the Folks Back Home

KANKOOKYAKU

tourists

Sylvia's Restaurant in the heart of Manhattan's Harlem district serves delectable American soul food to the local community. Survey the establishment and you'll notice tables piled high with Down-Home Fried Chicken, Yummie-Yummie Rum Cake, and Sylvia's World Famous Talked About Bar-B-Que Ribs Special with her Sweet and Spicy Sauce. These days, you'll also see a number of unfamiliar faces peering out from behind the Cow Peas and Rice and Okra and Tomato Gumbo: bus loads of Japanese visitors. As Sylvia's has found out, in New York as in most major cities around the world, the Japanese *kankookyaku*, or tourist, has arrived.

From Honolulu to Heidelberg, the image of camera-clicking Louis Vuitton-toting Japanese tourists has become the exaggerated stereotype for visitors from abroad. Their favorite travel destinations include, for example, the United States, South Korea, Hong Kong, Taiwan, Singapore, France, and Switzerland. With a yen for yen, tour operators have been feverishly devising imaginative public rela-tions campaigns

to entice the traveling Japanese, who tend to spend substantially more than their American counterparts. Scotland is promoting itself as the ideal place for the Japanese to sip Scotch whisky and play golf. England is selling its Yorkshire Moors as the romantic land of the Brontë sisters and *Wuthering Heights*. And Israel is pitching the Dead Sea as a sure beauty cure—it even dressed El Al flight attendants in kimono to inaugurate commercial flights between Israel and Japan.

Now that a honeymoon abroad has become practically *de rigueur* among Japanese, Alaska is promoting its northern lights to newlyweds by claiming that a marriage consummated under the lights will be long and happy. The French region of Brittany is encouraging Japanese honeymooners to dress up in folkloric costumes and repeat their wedding vows to the tune of local music. Not to be outdone, Paris is offering young Japanese couples a bridal speech by a real French marquis and a videotape of the affair to show the folks back home.

How do you make Japanese tourists feel at home away from home? Pamper them with the same efficiency and friendly service they find in Japan (remember to smile a lot). Shuttle them from airport to hotel. Supply them with Japanese-language menus, green tea, and maybe even lightweight Japanese pajamas. Provide couples with two single beds, not one double bed. Finally, make sure their accommodations include bathtubs, not merely showers, and be prepared for them to splash liberally outside the tub, as is common in Japan. The splashing can lead to such flooding that one Western hotel catering to Japanese has installed drainage pipes in the bathroom floors and alarms that go off when the water from the bath in, say, room 603 soaks through to room 503.

Japanese tourists are used to living in secure surroundings, carrying large wads of cash, and leaving bags unattended. As a result, they are sitting ducks for theft, especially in cities known for occasional outbreaks of Japan-bashing. One classic scam involves a huckster (known to the Japanese as the "bagman") who carries a paper bag containing a wine bottle filled with colored water; he or she knocks into a Japanese tourist, lets the container drop, and then demands that the Japanese victim pay dearly for having smashed a bottle of precious French wine.

Despite safety concerns and the language barrier, Japanese tourists are increasingly willing to venture beyond the standard group tours of Paris, London, or New York. At the same time, many still cling to fixed notions of where to go and why. For instance, there's the famous story of a Japanese lady who traveled to Switzerland to satisfy a lifelong yearning to visit the famed peaks of Mont Blanc. What she failed to realize, however, is that Mont Blanc is in France.

So Cute You Could Gag

KAWAII

cute

Terminal cuteness is smothering Japan. Smiley-face buttons and rainbow stickers may send chills down the spine of any hard-boiled Western teenager, but they're apt to make even an impassive sumo wrestler melt into sugar and squeal *"Kawaii!"* (translation: "How cute!").

A kawaii-addict is inclined at the most advanced age to amass shameless quantities of puppy dog posters and Snoopy bags. He or she tends to gravitate to perky teenage singers decked out in velvety party dresses whose main vocal accomplishment is the ability to show lots of teeth and giggle on cue.

In marketing terms, kawaii translates into big business for those cute enough to cash in on the phenomenon. For instance, Japan's popular female cartoon character Hello Kitty may look like your average airhead cat, but this puss knows how to spell profits. Miss Kitty's backers have shrewdly developed Hello Kitty purses, baby nail clippers, cotton puffs, orange soda, gelatin, jam, children's shoes, and bubble gum.

The Japanese high temple of cuteness is, of course, an American import: Tokyo Disneyland, the home of Goofy-san, Mickey-san, and a kimono-clad Minnie. Each year, millions of eager visitors stream into the amusement park, which is now generally ranked the country's number one "date course" (the ideal place to take a date). Believe it or not, in one survey a majority of Japanese women rated a visit to Tokyo Disneyland the single greatest pleasure-giving experience of their lives. Thanks to slogans such as "Mickey Beats Skiing," even die-hard athletes now opt to spend their precious vacation time with a cartoon mouse.

Has Japanese kawaii really run amuck? Just ask Japan's Sanyo Mutual Savings Bank, which decided to change its name to one which would evoke more of a "cute, lovable image." Welcome, dear depositors, to the newly re-christened, ever-so-adorable . . . Tomato Bank.

What's Blond, Blue-eyed, and Speaks Japanese?

GAIJIN TARENTO

"foreign talent"

Teach an otherwise average American to speak flawless Japanese, put him or her in front of a Japanese TV camera, and what do you get? A *gaijin tarento*, of course, meaning a foreign media personality who charms millions of adoring Japanese fans with the ability to schmooze on cue in the local lingo.

Two of Japan's top "foreign talents" are surprisingly similar: both are squeaky clean midwestern Mormons named Kent who graduated from Brigham Young University and originally came to Japan to work as missionaries—Kent Gilbert and Kent Derricott.

Attorney Kent Gilbert's career as a media star took off after he appeared on a popular Japanese game show and dazzled the public with his good looks, affable manner, and startling command of Japanese. Since then, Kento-san, as Gilbert is known, has dished out homespun American commentary on talk shows, game shows, and radio programs and has lectured at wedding receptions. He has also penned best-sellers, starred in a TV series, and (moving from fast talk to fast food) even launched an ill-fated Mexican food chain that took a permanent siesta after a couple of years in business. Gilbert also became involved in a spiffy foreign-language school where students take lessons in Rolls-Royce limousines, Ferrari sports cars, and other fancy foreign automobiles. Kent Gilbert's success prompted the blond, blue-eyed, bespectacled Kent Derricott to join the talking-foreigner bandwagon. Derricott, who used to run an export company in Japan, has cut his own rock and roll album and regularly delivers witty repartee on television and radio waves across the country.

Another household name (in Japanese homes, at least) is Dave Spector, a flamboyant foreign talent who hails from Chicago and used to write for *National Lampoon*. Challenging the oh-so-wholesome image of the others, Spector reportedly first appeared on the Japanese tube with bleached blond hair. In one recent quiz show, Spector submerged himself in near-boiling water in a "hot springs" bath while the quiz show contestants tried to guess how long he could hold out (or pass out). Spector's other credits include a regular magazine column, more than twelve books, a Japanese comedy show, and a talent agency.

To many Japanese, foreign talents are both elusively foreign and, because of their gift for gab, immediately accessible. Capitalizing on this appeal, Japanese advertising companies feature non-Japanese in almost one-third of their television spots and create commercials featuring Western stars who, with a bit of coaching, can even pitch products in the local tongue. Michael J. Fox, punning artfully in Japanese, calls the Integra automobile a "cool car." Sylvester Stallone vows to Japanese TV audiences, "My heart and Ito Ham." Celebrity-hunk Arnold Schwarzenegger dresses up as a genie and pushes a vitamin-fortified drink by exclaiming in Japanese, "I'm O.K.!" James Coburn promotes Lark cigarettes with the mystifying one-liner: "Speak Lark." (Don't ask what the slogan means, just buy the stuff.) Fearing that Western audiences might find these lucrative but silly advertisements unbecoming for a true star, many American celebrities insist on "Japan Only" clauses in their contracts, which impose heavy penalties if the commercials are broadcast outside of Japan.

Another twist on the foreign talent boom is the craze for Japanese personalities (especially women) who are able to speak pristine English. The so-called bilingals (short for "bilingual gals"; in Japanese, *bairingyaru*) have usually lived abroad and then returned home to flaunt their linguistic talents in the mass media. For instance, the popular Tokyo music station J-Wave features bilingual anchors who deftly slip in and out of English and Japanese. Of course, the English on J-Wave is probably lost on most Japanese listeners, but the seductive sound of the language is still considered *kakko ii*, or "really neat."

Are foreign talents articulate ambassadors helping to promote international understanding, or mere multilingual media mavens? For the answer to this and other questions . . . stay tuned.

No Pianos, Pets, or Foreigners

KOKUSAIKA

internationalization

A Japanese advertisement for an English language school shows an affable American fellow trying valiantly to chat up a meek Japanese lady in English; unable to respond, the woman panics, freezes, and turns to stone. As this modern Medusa tale suggests, many Japanese are still somewhat insular. To change all this, Japanese industrialists, politicians, and journalists have been talking for years about striving for *kokusaika*, a buzzword from the early 1980s meaning "internationalization."

On the diplomatic and economic fronts, Japan is becoming more international every day. Japan's Crown Prince is married to a Harvard-educated Japanese career diplomat. Government leaders are brushing up on their English. Subways are humming with commuters plugged into foreign-language conversation tapes. Businesses are expanding overseas and hiring Americans (and not just for English proofreading). Foreign loanwords have infested the Japanese language—for instance, "dan-pa" (dance party), "hi-so" (high society) "wa-pro" (word processor) and "young-egg" (young executive). Branch campuses of American colleges, such as Temple University Japan, are popping up in Japan, and branches of Japanese institutions, such as Tokyo International University, are cropping up stateside. Japan's Makudonarudo—McDonald's—is churning out real American burgers, while other chains are pushing Japanese-style "rice burgers"—meat patties on buns made of rice. Tourism is booming. Michael Jackson is a demigod. *Kokusaika* is still the word of the hour: successfully pitch a product or person as "international" and you've got a winner on your hands.

Resisting the impulse to internationalize are those Japanese who cling to the notion that Japan is unique and should stay that way. Some even pursue *nihonjinron*, the study of how the Japanese differ from other humans. In the same vein, certain Japanese are still reluctant to approach, interact with, or (horrors!) marry *gaijin* (meaning "foreigners" or, literally, "outsiders"). As a result, gaijin can easily be made to feel isolated in this small island-nation. For instance, in more remote towns, Japanese youngsters have been known to point to foreigners, cry out "gaijin!" from a safe distance, and run for cover.

Moreover, Japanese real estate agents are infamous for turning away foreigners in search of housing. (What would a Japanese landlady say to foreign tenants who trampled on her tatami mat floors with their dirty sneakers?!) A classic real estate posting even advises: "No pianos, pets, or foreigners." Similarly, Tokyo taxi drivers, although considerably more polite than their Western counterparts, are renowned for being curiously unable to see or stop for gaijin passengers. The standard explanation is that Japanese cabbies assume that foreigners live closer than Japanese to the city centers and therefore tend to go shorter distances and pay lower fares. A more cynical explanation is that the drivers simply prefer to avoid the bother of dealing with non-Japanese-speaking aliens.

Many Japanese seem keenly interested—some say obsessed—with the outside world and with what foreigners think of them. From the gaijin's point of view, it's encouraging when locals want to "internationalize" and connect with the rest of the world. But it would also be nice if, after all the talk of kokusaika is finished for the day, a foreigner living in Tokyo could, hassle-free, hail a cab home.

One Old Lady in a Cashmere Overcoat

FUROOSHA

the homeless

Orderly Japan has no *furoosha*, or homeless people. Or does it? Consider the following account of a New Yorker who took up temporary residence in Tokyo:

"It was 5 a.m. one rainy morning and I lay curled up next to my space-heater, snoozing away on my futon. Dreaming of cherry blossoms and tea ceremonies, I ignored the muffled noises coming from the alley outside my door. After all, I had long since grown accustomed to noisy businessmen stumbling home at all hours.

"But as the din from outside my bedroom grew, I grudgingly raised one eyelid and slid open the screen separating my bedroom from the tiny kitchen next door. Glancing toward the kitchen window, I reassured myself that no one was there.

" 'Tokyo may not always be quiet,' I thought, 'but at least it's safe.'

"Just then, I spotted someone squatting in a dark corner of my kitchen, rocking back and forth. Years of living in Manhattan paid off immediately

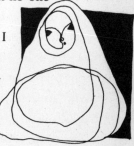

and I did what any true New Yorker would have done in a similar situation: I panicked.

"I sprang to my feet and struck a pose that I had seen in a recent sumo wrestling match. Unfortunately, even in the dark I am not a particularly imposing figure. To make matters worse, I sleep in the buff.

"The mysterious intruder continued to rock back and forth menacingly and mumbled something in high-pitched Japanese. What does a helpless foreigner do in this kind of situation? My guidebook had been silent on the topic of breaking and entering. And having been told that Tokyo was perfectly safe, I hadn't bothered to jot down an emergency telephone number.

" '*Tomodachi, tomodachi*,' cried the intruder. Surprisingly, it was a female voice, and the words meant "friend, friend." Though it was too dark to make out her face, she appeared to be covered in old blankets.

"Reasoning that the uninvited visitor might be some homicidal maniac, I tried to yell, 'Leave my apartment at once!' But since my well-meaning Japanese teacher had taught me only the most respectful forms of the language, I ended up shouting: 'It is rude of me to disturb you, but if it's not too much trouble, might you kindly withdraw from here?'

" '*Tomodachi! tomodachi*!' she pleaded.

"Suddenly, I wondered if she was possibly an acquaintance of mine. Maybe a fellow foreigner who had missed the last train from Tokyo Station.

" 'Who are you?' I asked. Whoever she was, I could now see that she was soaked and shivering.

" '*Tomodachi*,' she insisted. '*Hana o motte kimashita*.' I understood this to mean, 'I have brought you a flower.'

" 'A flower?' I thought. 'Is this some crazed Japanese botanist? Or just a cold, pathetic homeless woman who wandered into my unlocked apartment after being thrown out of the nearby train station?'

"As I began to conclude that the latter was probably closest to the truth, she leapt up, lunged for my best (and only) winter overcoat, threw it around her shoulders, and vanished through the front door.

"That evening, before turning out the light, I pondered the fate of the homeless in Japan. I also remembered to double-lock my front door—at least, that is, until I returned to the safety of New York City.

"The local police authorities later assured me that no homeless people live in Japan. Except, perhaps, for one old lady wearing my cashmere overcoat."

Come Hell or Higher Education

SHIKEN JIGOKU

exam hell

"Sleep four hours, pass; sleep five hours, fail." Students who choose to ignore this Japanese proverb may flunk their exams and miss the so-called escalator, or fast-track to success. The quality of Japanese education can be heavenly, but study-holic students pay the price by undergoing *shiken jigoku*, or "exam hell," a battery of pressure-filled tests that culminate in the rigorous university entrance examinations.

A Japanese candidate's future hangs in the balance during exam hell since top scores lead to the top schools that lead to the top companies that generally hire for life. The track begins as early as preschool, when some precocious toddlers compete for admission to exclusive elementary schools by marching to music, clenching their fists on cue, or exhibiting other early signs of genius. In later years, most tests focus on English, Japanese, math, science, and social studies; they consist of multiple-choice or short-answer questions and require memorizing mountains of factual minutiae.

From primary school until college (which, unlike in America, is a blissful four-year break between exam hell and the rigors of employment), many supplement regular school with *juku*, meaning private after-school or weekend instruction that is geared to cramming for the scholastic judgment day. Since admission to some juku is contingent on passing an entrance exam, youngsters may have to cram to get into cram school. On an average day, an eleven-year-old might attend school for eight hours, then head off to juku for ninety minutes, and finally come home to buckle down to a late night of homework.

Behind many exam-hell success stories is a doting *kyooiku mama*, or "education mama," who falls somewhere between a classic Jewish mother and a stage mom. While her husband is busy at the office, the education mama selflessly devotes herself to the academic success of her offspring by conferring with teachers, taking notes for the kids when they are absent from class, registering them for exams, sitting up with them as they cram, and cooking endless bowls of buckwheat noodles—the Japanese equivalent of chicken soup.

All this studying produces results: not only do an extraordinarily high percentage of high school students graduate, but Japanese students are among the world's best in math and science, and the country boasts a 99 percent literacy rate. As for study habits, students learn early on how to *gambaru* (try hard and persist). Unsuccessful university applicants show off their ability to persist when they slog away for one or two years studying intensely to retake their exams.

Proponents of Japan's educational system point out that

admission to schools and universities is based purely on merit (except, that is, for the expensive cram schools) and that teachers enjoy high status and good pay. Even first-graders stand and bow when the *sensei* (meaning "teacher" or, literally, "elder") enters the classroom. Yet, critics call the system a stifling pressure cooker that sacrifices creativity for conformity. In average classes of thirty-nine students, pupils follow a nationally prescribed curriculum, are kept on the same track the teacher's lecture with questions or opinions. In addition, hairstyles and dress code are often dictated; typical attire is regulation-length skirts and dark blue boys' uniforms complete with big brass buttons and high collars. These militaristic outfits seem eerily appropriate for children who are put through Japan's so-called *juken sensoo*, or "exam preparation war."

One sign of the national preoccupation with academic achievement is that many students write down the very same prayers when they visit local shrines: "Please let me pass my exams." Keeping up with the times, one shrine now reportedly allows pupils to fax their exam-related wishes. The lucky few whose prayers are answered gain admission to Tokyo University (academic heaven) or a few other elite institutions and are thus assured an escalator ride up to the top ranks of Japanese industry or government. At the other extreme, those who repeatedly get burned in exam hell may have to take a different escalator: the one going down.

II
the BUSINESS WORLD

All Work and No Play

SARARIIMAN

"salaryman"

"**Y**ou're fired!" These are words that the Japanese white-collar worker, or "salaryman," seldom hears even in this time of economic cutbacks, but the life of Japan's economic beast of burden is no easier for it. Imagine having two weeks of vacation a year written into your contract and not being able to enjoy even one. Or being expected to stay late at the office whether or not there's work to do and then having to go out drinking with your colleagues. Every night. Add to this an average commute of three hours a day spent on your feet in a tightly packed train, and you have a pretty good idea of what life is like for the typical salaryman.

The word "salaryman" was coined after World War II to distinguish salaried employees from blue-collar workers who were paid on a daily basis. The "man" in "salaryman" is basically accurate since the vast majority of Japan's white-collar workers are men. Since the end of the war, women have generally been barred from management-track positions and often

wind up as professional "tea ladies," serving refreshments to the men who may have been her classmates and to others in Japan's companies.

For the most part, today's salarymen still enjoy lifetime employment, promotion on a purely seniority basis, and long, long hours. Add to this the deadening commute and compulsory after-hours socializing, and you have a recipe for stress. The typical salaryman often returns home after 11 p.m.—in enough time to take a bath, have a snack, and hit the hay, but far too late to tuck in the kids. Moreover, at some point during his career he may be transferred to another city "temporarily"—one to three years. In such cases, rather than disrupt his children's studies by making them change schools, he may choose to separate from his family, thus becoming a so-called business bachelor.

At the outermost extreme, salarymen in perpetual overdrive have succumbed to *karooshi*, or death from overwork. In such cases, it is small comfort that some companies now even provide company cemeteries for employees and their loved ones who have shown an "undying" loyalty to the firm—the ultimate symbol of a cradle-to-grave attitude taken by some employers with respect to their employees. Under fire from groups such as the National Defense Counsel for Victims of Death from Overwork, the Japanese government has launched a major study into the quality of life in the Japanese workplace.

If salaryman life is such a grind, why don't Japan's stoic workers simply quit their jobs in search of greener pastures? One answer is a strong company loyalty that is reflected in a salaryman's everyday speech. On his first day of work, he begs his new colleagues to "please accept my humble consideration in the future." From then on, he introduces himself as an extension of the company—for example, "I am Tanaka Corporation's Suzuki." And at retirement, he may tearfully tell co-workers, "You have all taken such good care of me!"

Financial and social pressures also keep many salarymen wedded to their companies. Job-hopping, while appealing to some, can mean accepting a cut in status, income, and private pension, all of which tend to be tied to the number of years of company service. Some businesses are also reluctant to hire a salaryman who has presumably shown disloyalty by bailing out from his former employer. And switching jobs takes guts in a society which prizes conformity to the group.

Grim though salaryman life may seem, it appears to be slowly changing for the better. Working conditions are improving and, especially in light of the recent downturn in Japan's economy, working hours are getting shorter. The Labor Ministry has even instituted a poster campaign designed to encourage workers to take more of their vacation time. Commercial banks are leading the way, having abolished weekend work, and some companies are actually encouraging employees to leave the office early. For example, one major computer company has instituted a "no-overtime Wednesday"; at 5 p.m. a cheery voice over the intercom chirps, "Let's all go home now!"

Such improvements in working conditions partly result from the new outlook of Japanese youth, who are derisively called "beansprouts" because they grow tall but lack stamina. Free from the memory of postwar hardships, Japan's "beansprouts" realize that all work and no play makes Yoichiro an unhappy boy.

Whatever one might think of salaryman life, Japan's indomitable white-collar workers have clearly generated the country's so-called economic miracle. Ironically, while Japan's impressive productivity has expanded the country's share of the world pie, the majority of salarymen usually get home too late to enjoy their piece in peace.

A Feminist's Nightmare

OL

"office lady"

She walks, talks, smiles, bows, and even serves tea. She comes complete with a snappy blue-and-white uniform for office work and a dazzling wardrobe for nights on the town. They call her the "OL," or "office lady," and she is everywhere in Japanese companies, marking time performing routine clerical tasks until the happy day when she marries and quits her job. It's a feminist's nightmare.

OLs epitomize the fate of so many Japanese working women: relegated to slow-track jobs with no job description and little chance for career advancement while their male counterparts enjoy management-track positions. Basically glorified receptionists, OLs at all stages of their careers tend to carry out low-level tasks such as photocopying, answering the phones, greeting customers, running errands, and, of course, serving tea. Paradoxically, while their professional possibilities are virtually nil, OLs enjoy more freedom, independence, and cold cash than ever before.

Because many OLs live with their parents and assume that their future husbands will support them, they tend to treat their salaries as disposable income. As a result, fleets of free-frolicking office ladies embark on lavish shopping and dining expeditions, international vacations, and other forms of pricey self-indulgence. Nicknamed the "single nobility," the OL has been a boon to Japan's cosmetic, fashion, and travel industries. At most of the world's top vacation destinations, one is bound to run into the OL, whose vacation plans invariably include sunbathing, sightseeing, and spending.

The typical OL is (outside the workplace, at least) assertive, fun-loving, well-educated, ostentatious, and very free—until, that is, she weds. At that point, her paternalistic employers and watchful parents often pressure her to quit work and assume the family responsibilities that will become the primary focus of her life. Before marriage, an OL is said to divide her boyfriends into distinct groups: "Asshii-kun" ("Mr. Wheels"), who drives her around; "Messhii-kun" ("Mr. Meals"), who invites her to expensive restaurants; "Mitsugu-kun ("Mr. Sugar Daddy"), who lavishes furs and jewelry; "Narabi-kun" (Mr. Line Up), who patiently waits on long ticket lines for her; "Kiipu-kun" ("Mr. Keep"), who is a sensible person to marry and whom she keeps in the wings in case her true love slips away; and the elusive "Honmei-kun" ("Mr. Real"), her true love.

In the late 1980s, OLs were said to be *bodikon*, or "body conscious," meaning unabashedly committed to showing off their figures in clothes so tight-fitting that they were second only to nature. The 1990s have brought a new trend to free-thinking OLs: the desire to engage, uninhibitedly, in racetrack betting, golf, hard drinking, pinball, and mah-jongg—diversions traditionally reserved for middle-aged men, or *oyaji*. The OL who dares to enjoy such male pastimes is, therefore, nicknamed the "oyaji-gal," i.e., "the middle-aged-man girl." Catering to the new surge of female customers, some race courses now provide such additional amenities as pink-tiled restrooms for women and gleefully report that oyaji-gals now comprise a full two-thirds of the clientele. Jockeys have become idols among loyal female followers. And pachinko parlors such as The Pyramid have started to create "women-only" sections that are cleaner and brighter than the rest of the shop, that are serviced by attendants dressed in fashionable checkerboard vests, and that offer prizes intended to appeal to Japanese women, such as Mickey Mouse dolls and fresh fruit.

"Oyaji-gal" was coined by a young female cartoonist whose comic strip, "Sweet Spot," depicts office lady life and gives fictional OL characters the chance to talk back to their bosses. Assertiveness also appears in the popular new card game "No-Men-Allowed Workplace." Players are subjected to sexual harassment and then take turns wreaking revenge on their lecherous bosses by, for example, kicking them between the legs or contacting the bosses' wives. Also feeding off the OL phenomenon is the successful magazine *Hanako*—the typical name for the girl next door—which has developed a loyal following among the so-called *Hanako-zoku*, or "Hanako tribe" (i.e., the OLs).

The Japanese media like to point to the improved status of women—to the new *Onna no Jidai*, or "Age of Women" in which more women (or so-called Madonnas) run for parliament and fight for the rights of their sex. Whether this continues to be true in a declining economy remains to be seen. In any case, during business hours most office ladies are still constrained by male chauvinism in the workplace, otherwise known as the invisible "pink curtain."

The Big Brass

SHACHOO

company president

Japanese chief executive officers (CEOs) generally don't impose their egos on their companies or earn astronomical sums. But lest there be any question about who's in charge, Japanese employees quickly learn to address their revered leader by prestigious title rather than by name. They call him or her *shachoo*, meaning, quite simply, "Mr. (or Mrs.) Company President."

Who is the typical shachoo? A man in his late fifties who entered his company directly after graduating from an elite college, was pegged early on as a corporate golden boy, and has spent the last thirty years slogging his way up the corporate ladder. While few women are given the chance to rise as executives in large companies, there are tens of thousands of female shachoo, many of whom sought career advancement by launching their own businesses. With a strong work ethic and familial sense of responsibility to their employees, company presidents typically keep a low profile while stressing teamwork, group harmony, and consensus-building. In many cases, rather than managing the company, they concentrate on maintaining good relationships both inside and outside the firm. This may mean officiating at employee weddings, giving speeches at directors' funerals, paying social calls on customers, sipping tea with suppliers, or bowing to government bureaucrats. Many Japanese CEOs strive to please their employees and customers rather than their shareholders, who, they assume, are naturally behind them.

Cushioned by Japan's system of lifetime employment, company presidents enjoy relatively stable positions (on average, they serve an eight-year stint) in contrast to their American counterparts, who are more likely to be ousted by pesky boards of directors or to jump ship when a competing company dangles an attractive corporate carrot. Should their firms face scandal or financial ruin, Japanese chiefs are inclined to resign voluntarily—whether or not they were at fault—rather than risk being dismissed in disgrace. Japanese presidents also feel less pressure than their American counterparts to produce immediate results; in Japan, CEO performances are judged on a long-term (three to five years) basis in contrast to the yearly or quarterly evaluation common in the United States.

With a firm sense of obligation to the corporate family rather than an eye exclusively to the bottom line, Japanese presidents accept voluntary pay cuts instead of laying off workers and, even in prosperous times, earn far less than Americans in similar positions. Japanese bosses are paid only about sixteen times what their average workers make, while American chief executives may pull in over eighty-five times the average worker's salary. Many Japanese believe that inflated

CEO salaries hurt company morale by distancing presidents from their workers; profits, they say, should be plowed back into the business rather than into presidents' pockets or shareholders' hands via dividends.

Critics complain that Japanese CEOs don't actually *do* anything and are mere extensions of a corporate group who are unwilling or unable to act with voices of their own. Some also observe that while Japanese presidents earn less than American executives, they make up the difference with handsome perks such as free golf club memberships, chauffeur-driven cars, vacation retreats, health clubs, generous retirement packages, and unlimited expense accounts for lavish entertaining. Japanese top management can send an expense account through the roof on a nightly basis in exorbitantly priced "hostess bars," where customers enjoy the company of flirtatious bar hostesses, flowing saké, and other late-night lubricants.

The question of whether Japanese presidents are underpaid may in any case be moot. After all, working into the wee hours seven days a week, a shachoo might ask himself: "What's the point of making any more money if by the time I leave the office to spend it the stores are all closed and I'm ready to collapse?"

Spartan Love

SEMPAI/KOOHAI

senior/junior hierarchy

Addressing an older Japanese colleague, a naive junior associate coolly commanded: "Pass me that ashtray." "Get it yourself!" fired back the smoldering co-worker to his ashen-faced junior. "Don't forget, I'm your senior!" In hierarchical Japan, the distinction between juniors and seniors—called *koohai* and *sempai*—is as sharp as the division between hot and cold. Junior workers who forget this may risk coming under heated attack by their elders or receiving icy stares from their peers.

In many Japanese colleges, where studying takes a back seat to socializing, the junior-senior relationship plays itself out in the form of student-run clubs. There, the younger members defer to upperclassmen by, for example, pouring beer for them during all-night drinking sessions when seniors feel the urge for such peon company. Rather than calling elder club members by name, juniors often address them as simply "sempai" and use the polite form of speech (no abrupt grammatical endings, please). As big brother or big sister, the senior is free to address his or her underlings casually, which means lopping off the honorific *san* at the end of a name.

As graduation approaches, job-hunting students often look to their seniors to smooth their career paths. Acting as go-between for the company and college, seniors might go out for coffee with their former junior classmates, playing up the company to the students and vice-versa. If the firm offers employment to the junior, the senior takes on a new role: he or she must guard the candidate jealously from offers from competing employers.

Once corporate life begins, the senior-junior relationship holds strong. Seniors act as mentors, showing their juniors the company ropes, helping to train them, and introducing them to clients. When invited by seniors to go drinking after work, juniors generally succumb to the same pressure to oblige that they felt in college. For Japanese businesses, this senior-junior dynamic is a source of stability. Lifetime employment keeps the firm in place, while the rigid pecking order keeps the place firm.

Like a watchful older sibling, the Japanese senior has one protective eye out for obedient juniors and another critical eye on juniors who stray. Even when a senior is tough with his or her junior, the two still depend on, and somehow care for, the other. It's a kind of Spartan love.

Good Faith Counts for a Lot

BENGOSHI

attorney

The Japanese often conduct business without a legal practitioner, turning to their *bengoshi*, or attorney, only as a last resort. When a dispute arises and the lawyer is called in, the aim is to patch up a disagreement, not leap into a lawsuit. The bengoshi will do his or her utmost to placate, conciliate, and arbitrate—but, for heaven's sake, not litigate.

Some claim that Japanese are by nature nonlitigious, seeking at all costs to preserve *wa*, or harmony, and maintain long-term relationships. Litigation, they say, is an embarrassing admission that the conciliation process has failed, and a court of law is an all-too-public place for feuding parties to air their private grievances. Others suggest a more practical explanation for the Japanese reluctance to enforce their rights in a legal forum: the scarcity of Japanese lawyers. Many young people take the state law exam, but the number of candidates who are allowed to pass is so limited that a severe shortage of practicing lawyers, prosecutors, and judges has developed. With so few judges and lawyers to handle cases, courts are clogged and lawsuits routinely drag on for anywhere from two to ten years.

Japan survives with so few bengoshi largely because non-lawyers perform what seems to outsiders like legal work. For instance, patent specialists, tax practitioners, and court scriveners are not licensed attorneys. Similarly, many corporations have in-house legal departments staffed with nonlawyers who studied law but never took or passed the bar. Within companies, senior management, rather than attorneys, negotiate contracts, which tend to be short, sketchy documents. Since Japanese agreements are flexible and based on trust, businessmen don't feel compelled to spell out every contingency in excruciating detail. The idea is that, if circumstances change, the parties will simply sit down over green tea and hammer out a solution. Good faith counts for a lot.

Revered in Japanese society as part of an elite club of brilliant barristers, a bengoshi is accorded the high honor of being addressed as "teacher." Lawyers are so rare that their clients actually court them and try to stay in their good graces by offering them gifts—an ironic twist on the feverish efforts at client development common among some Western legal talent. Moreover, because so few candidates pass the bar, women who do so can rise in the legal profession. Bengoshi tend to be sole practioners and generalists, although some have now formed larger law firms that specialize in complex commercial matters for major international corporations.

Japanese lawyers are free to hire foreign attorneys and work alongside American counsel in a number of U.S. jurisdictions. In contrast, most non-Japanese lawyers have been allowed to practice in Japan only since 1987, and then only if they have at least five year's experience in their home jurisdictions. In addition, foreign law firms in Japan may still not practice Japanese law or employ bengoshi to advise foreign clients. Such restrictions may reflect the Japanese fear that unleashing American lawyers in Japan could taint a non-contentious society with nests of nettlesome attorneys.

Nevertheless, in the past few years some Japanese have become more willing to assert their legal rights even at the expense of appearing adversarial. For instance, Japanese women have recently turned to lawyers to advise and defend them in ground-breaking sexual harassment suits against employers. As bengoshi continue to fight injustice in the public forum, the Japanese public may become increasingly conscious of their legal rights and dispense with some misgivings about resorting to the legal process. Only then, for better or worse, can legal eagles soar.

Don't Leave Home Without It

MEISHI

business card

What has four corners, fits in your pocket, and holds the key to identity and self-esteem? The answer is the Japanese business card, known locally as the *meishi*.

Exchanging meishi is serious business in Japan. *Everyone* has one and is poised to produce it at a moment's notice: the high school sophomore, the Buddhist monk, the gas station attendant . . . even the gangster. And, of course, the businessman. According to one report, twelve million of these little beauties are swapped daily in Japan.

First used in Japan in the beginning of the nineteenth century, many meishi are still based on the Western model, meaning name and rank in sober black lettering, sometimes with an English translation on the reverse. More personalized cards also abound, so whatever your needs, there's a meishi just for you. There are plastic-coated, waterproof meishi for swimmers; smaller meishi with rounded corners for dainty women; recycled meishi for environmentalists; aromatic meishi for romantics; and, for the bar hostess, a meishi that becomes supple and pliable in the warmth of your hand. For Japanese born with silver spoons in their mouths, there are now even gold meishi.

The student of meishi protocol quickly learns the basics of presenting, accepting, and storing the handy card. Stand up, bow slightly, and, with a snap of the wrist worthy of a squash pro, present your meishi with one hand. After receiving a card in return for your own, pause to scrutinize it earnestly (pretend to admire the bearer's impressive title, whether or not you actually read Japanese). If you are not handed a card in return for your own, you have just been given the classic Japanese brush-off. Worse still, tearing up someone's business card is a symbolic form of homicide.

Remember: a tidy meishi is a happy meishi. Don't even think about folding the card or scribbling a note on its flip side (at least not in the presence of its donor). Carefully organize your cards by category and lovingly store them in the individual plastic pouches of special file books.

Why all this fuss about business cards? The answer, in part, is that in a strictly hierarchical society they let the recipient know how much politeness and respect to accord the bearer. One glance at the title on a meishi and most Japanese know what level of speech to use and how low to bow. More importantly, business cards afford the Japanese conformist a vital sense of identity and belonging. In fact, according to the group Well Aging Japan, some Japanese executives become so dependent on their meishi that they experience severe depression and loneliness when they are forced to relinquish the card at retirement. One recommended remedy is to begin handing out private, non-company name cards well before retirement to avoid the embarrassment of a meishi-less existence.

Meishi also serve more unusual functions. For instance, at some restaurants a customer who is short of cash can avoid washing the dishes by simply leaving a business card with the cashier and paying later. Moreover, at one particular shrine dedicated to "people wishing for weddings," some practical-minded visitors have reportedly abandoned the custom of leaving red ribbons at the entryway and deposit their business cards instead. Meishi abuse is also on the rise. For example, one scam is to pretend to be connected to an influential politician by stealing his or her meishi and showing it to others. (Flaunting other people's meishi is a form of name-dropping in Japan.) To prevent such abuse, some prominent Japanese now mark the recipient's name and the date on each card they hand out.

A foreigner in Japan without a meishi is like an American without an American Express card. Don't leave home without it.

To Bow or Not to Bow

AISATSU

greeting

A t precisely ten o'clock one Sunday morning, a Japanese lady appeared at the home of her American physician. Surprised to see her, he asked whether she had come about a medical complaint, and she indicated that she hadn't. Somewhat perplexed by the visit, he invited her in and offered her tea, which she gratefully accepted. A short while later, she thanked him, got up, and left. The next day, the doctor noticed a sign in his office which read: "On Sundays, doctor's visiting hours start at ten a.m." His Japanese patient, he suddenly realized, had misinterpreted this to mean "courtesy calls begin at ten a.m." In Japan, formal visits and greeting ceremonies, known as *aisatsu*, are a common way to cement personal and professional relationships.

In Japanese business circles, where networking is often the name of the game, savvy businessmen routinely perform aisatsu, which involves visiting clients (often with a nicely wrapped gift in hand) and asking for their "kind consideration (*i.e.*, business) in the future." When new company presidents assume

their posts, the first order of business is to zip around to all their business contacts in a frenzy of aisatsu. And aisatsu reaches a feverish pitch every year around New Year's, as greeting cards, visitors, and requests for "humble consideration" ricochet from doorstep to doorstep.

Essential to aisatsu is knowing how and whether to bow. Japanese commonly bow in situations where Westerners would shake hands, although Japanese who meet foreigners will increasingly shake hands, or bow and then shake hands. For the Westerner who wrestles with that age-old question, "to bow or not to bow?" there's a simple solution: follow the other person's lead. If you decide to take the plunge and bow, remember to keep your hands by your sides and feet together and bow from the waist. In ordinary encounters, bow only slightly; when being introduced to someone for the first time, bow lower; and when meeting an older person or someone who commands respect, bow very deeply. Just be careful that you don't throw out your back in the process or accidentally butt heads with the "bowee."

Whereas in American stores and restaurants, the common way to greet customers is often to mutter "Next!", the Japanese prefer a mere civilized greeting—"*Irasshaimase!*" ("Welcome!"). Sushi bar chefs and waiters enthusiastically sing out this greeting in unison at such a piercing decibel level that you may worry that the soy sauce bottles will crack. Belting out frequent rounds of irasshaimase takes such a toll that one inventive Japanese company has developed "greeting robots" that call out the greeting with indefatigable vocal chords.

Foreigners who want to make a splash when greeting

Japanese should consider learning the basic words for "hello." When meeting someone for the first time, say *"hajime-mashite"* ("our meeting has begun"). The Japanese expression for "good morning" literally translates as "it is early," while "good evening" translates as "it is evening." Hearing such expressions, sarcastic Westerners may be tempted to quip back, "Why, so it is!" Finally, different regions may have their own, local greetings. For instance, in Osaka, which is famous for producing no-nonsense businessmen, a common greeting among shopkeepers is: *"Mookarimakka?"* Rough translation: "Made any money lately?"

The Right Route

NEMAWASHI

preparing for business

When corporate types speak of *nemawashi*—literally, digging around the roots of a tree to prepare it for transplanting—they are not daydreaming about alternate careers as gardeners or plotting to take over lumber companies. Rather, they are referring to Japan's traditional decision-making process by consensus, where most formal proposals are preceded by feverish behind-the-scenes maneuvering.

Nemawashi typically involves discussing an issue informally with colleagues to secure their tacit assent and then circulating an internal proposal for others to criticize or approve with the stamp of a personalized red-ink seal. Nemawashi may also mean networking in the business community or seeking advance approvals from government officials.

The Japanese pursuit of consensus has been touted over the Western autocratic management style on the theory that the Japanese approach airs all sides of an issue, spreads around the risk-taking, and ensures that a plan

will be executed without a hitch. Nemawashi is also said to boost company morale and commitment by making employees feel part of a decision-making team. To skeptics, however, nemawashi merely creates the illusion of group participation while leaving the key decisions to a few select managers. Moreover, impatient foreigners accustomed to a quick "time is money" approach to getting things done may find nemawashi to be frustratingly time-consuming. Critics say that nemawashi also stifles creativity, since a Japanese executive cannot make a last-minute change inspired by a burst of innovative genius without first checking back with everyone up and down the line.

Businesses hoping to branch out and blossom in Japan should remember nemawashi and exercise enough preliminary arboreal spadework. It may be just the right route to root for.

The Web They Weave

KEIRETSU

affiliated companies

Japan calls it cultivating long-term business relationships; Japan's biggest trading partner, America, calls it an unfair trade barrier. Both are referring to *keiretsu*, or the enormous networks of interconnected companies that flourish in Japan.

Most major Japanese companies are likely to belong to a particular horizontal keiretsu, meaning a family of corporations ranging from trading houses to real estate and electronics companies fused together by cross-stock holdings, shared directors, and a central cash-rich company or bank standing in the wings to provide powerful financial backing. Companies also form so-called vertical (or production) keiretsu in which a limited number of preferred suppliers and distributors feed off a powerful corporation. Within a single keiretsu, company chairmen and presidents might meet regularly and coordinate everything from investment plans to political donations; one example is the famous "Friday Club," which reportedly convenes between noon and 1:30 p.m. on the second Friday of every month. The marriage of keiretsu-affiliated

companies is further strengthened through collaboration on research and production, through the transfer of executives from one company to another, and, in the most literal sense, even through keiretsu dating services.

Advocates of keiretsu argue that it makes good business sense and fosters corporate harmony, loyalty, and efficiency. With its emphasis on stable share-holding, the keiretsu is said to encourage long-term planning (in contrast to what many Japanese perceive as U.S. corporate shortsightedness) and full employment while minimizing both the risk of American-style hostile takeovers and the pressure to reap quick profits for impatient shareholders. Arguing that the keiretsu network is open to any foreign company that can meet Japanese cost and quality standards, some have suggested that, rather than complaining about the perceived inequities of the keiretsu system, Americans should rather try to emulate it at home.

For their part, some American critics of keiretsu have called the alliances invidious outgrowths of pre-World War II *zaibatsu*, meaning the family-owned industrial empires that once fueled Japanese military might. To many such critics, a keiretsu is simply a form of corporate collusion that impedes free and fair competition by squeezing foreign competitors out of Japanese markets and by leading to price-fixing and exclusive supply arrangements. Japanese companies have also been faulted for using keiretsu in America by, for example, purchasing the components for their U.S.-based automobile factories from an established network of Japanese suppliers.

Foreign pressure is steadily mounting to force Japan to beef up lax anti-trust laws, regulate cross share-holdings, and divulge the opaque alliances that spread throughout and beyond the enormous tentacles of the keiretsu networks. However, given the influence and power of Japanese industry and the prominence of the "OB" ("old boy network") in Japan, some insiders question whether the Japanese government could effectively unravel the keiretsu web even if it wanted to. To its harshest critics, Japan is really "Japan, Inc." and the Japanese Ministry of Finance is, after all, merely the government center branch of Nomura Securities.

Unemployment

ROONIN

the (unemployed) masterless samurai

Just yesterday, it seemed, Japan's economy was booming, job-hopping was becoming more common and unemployment was almost unthinkable. Today, however, the Japanese have entered what the press calls the "superglacial recruitment age." Because of economic hard times, the carefree job-hopper has been replaced by the so-called "roonin," meaning the samurai warrior who lacks a master, or, in modern terms, the unemployed graduate.

Given the Japanese policy of lifetime employment, companies that need to tighten their belts are far more likely to cut down on recruiting than to lay off workers. As a result, employment opportunities are drying up. This is bad news in a country where students have always expected to find work during the recruiting season and before graduation, where post-graduation employment opportunities are scarce, and where one's first job following graduation has enormous impact on the rest of one's career.

Fewer jobs also mean fewer

opportunities for career-minded women, who have struggled to find meaningful work in Japan in even the best of economic times. Employers who were only gradually warming up to the idea of hiring women for white-collar jobs are now retreating from this approach.

In the good old days when college seniors had the luxury of many offers of employment, new recruits used their favorable bargaining position to insist on work that did not involve the "three K's"—*kiken* (dangerous), *kitsui* (demanding), and *kitanai* (dirty). Feeding off this choosiness, recruitment magazines started to list job openings and offer advice to prospective workers. *Travail* advised job-hopping women on how best to quit a job; *Adapt* informed English-language readers about choice openings in Japanese companies; and *Recruit* drummed up enthusiasm for modern work that is personally satisfying. When jobs were still easy to come by, even short-handed *yakuza*, or Japanese gangsters, were not above taking out help-wanted ads for "general clerks" in the popular recruitment magazines.

Moreover, in the heyday of the booming Japanese economy, companies used many methods to attract the most qualified candidates while discouraging so-called "U-turn" employees (those who leave big city corporations for smaller hometown businesses). A few employers even wooed prospective employees with dream nights in Tokyo, vacation trips abroad, and access to membership resort clubs equipped with lavish sports and entertainment facilities. Using pop culture to entice employees, an electronic giant promoted itself through a company comic book. Taking a more refined approach, the

Renoir coffee shop posted its help-wanted notice next to the image of an attractive young girl painted by Renoir.

Today, in contrast, job-seekers cannot afford to be so choosy, but they are becoming more enterprising and persistent in their search for work. The Internet and electronic mail are fruitful new avenues where job-hunters can get into touch with possible employers. Maybe this development will encourage even computer-illiterate condidates to develop skills in using newfangled technology. At the extreme, a college student may even cut classes in order to stay home by the telephone in case a prospective employer decides to call and make that elusive offer. A growing number of mid-career job-seekers have decided to enhance their chances of finding good work by enrolling in night-classes in economics offered in Tokyo's main business district.

Once they find jobs, employees are increasingly realizing that, given today's precarious economy, job-hopping can be risky business. Rather than looking outside their companies, many prefer to remain where they are (even if the work is not entirely satisfying) and to seek opportunities within the corporation.

According to Japanese economists, Japan's unemployment rate is still the lowest in the industrialized world. This may be true, but it's small comfort for the roonin who finds himself driving a taxi, rather than taking one to work.

A Heaven for Drunks

NOMU

drink

"**G**o for it, Mr. Liver!" is the simply scrumptious Japanese hangover remedy made from oysters, ginger, and honey. You would drink it, too, if you were a Japanese worker subjected to incessant rounds of obligatory drinking with clients and colleagues. Japanese business associates routinely *nomu*, or "drink," together through the night to relieve stress, cement personal relationships, and, most importantly, talk shop.

After work, some Japanese go to special bars where they can store and retrieve their private bottles. Since most drunken chatter is excused in Japan, drinking parties are a chance for subordinates to tell their bosses what they really think and for executives to try out new ideas on potential clients. The pressure to indulge is so fierce that teetotalers risk being labeled as

tsukiai ga warui, or "connecting badly with others."

The etiquette when drinking beer, whiskey, or saké—the most common choices in business circles—is to pour for your neighbors, never for yourself, but to empty a

bottle only in your own glass. When someone else is pouring for you, stop talking and raise your glass with the thumb and forefingers of the right hand while grasping the base of the glass with the left hand. Don't forget to top off the ritual with a rousing toast of *kampai!*—"cheers!"

Beer, a nineteenth-century Western import, is the most popular Japanese drink; it flows freely at an employee's welcome reception, a goodbye gathering, and a *boonenkai*—the "forget-the-year" party held each December. One major beer company entices customers to its drinking establishment with the promise of "Beer Communication," while its competitor, Asahi Beer, has adopted the catchy slogan: "Live Asahi for Live People."

Saké, pronounced "sa-kay" (not "sa-key"), is the established drink for ceremonial and religious occasions such as Shinto festivals, weddings, and new year. Traditionally served in the wintertime from a ceramic flask warmed to 110 degrees, saké is a clear, smooth liquid. It tastes particularly delectable when the drinker is sidling up to the counter of a cozy neighborhood pub, soaking in a hot spring bath, or snuggled up with his or her loved one at home on a chilly winter evening.

Sometimes called "a heaven for drunks," Japan may have over two million alcoholics. Some say that Japanese are especially susceptible to liquor, and acquire a reddish pallor when drinking, because their bodies lack sufficient ALDH enzymes to break down alcohol. Typically, the last train from the city to the suburbs brims with red-faced commuters who themselves are brimming with an excess of alcohol which they contain with varying degrees of success. Despite the efforts of organizations such as the Non-Drinkers' Association, the Japanese Abstinence Federation, and the Japan Council on Alcohol Studies, alcohol consumption is still rising in Japan, while declining in many Western nations. Along with business drinkers, there are so-called kitchen drinkers, meaning lonely housewives who have turned to the bottle in desperation. Minors also have easy access to liquor through the country's many vending machines, although there is a growing movement to sober up this industry.

Japanese are becoming increasingly concerned about alcohol's ill effects, and so even die-hard drinkers are supplementing their usual intake with, for example, a variety of so-called vitamin drinks. Available from sources such as Tokyo's aptly named Energy Pool Bar, vitamin drinks such as Hard Work (with extra sugar and vitamin C) and Be-Can (with extra calcium from coral reefs) are said to facilitate physical labor. And for stamina when performing tedious desk jobs, there is Daily Work (with extract of ginkgo leaf) and Regain—for which the commercial asks, "Can you fight for twenty-four hours?"

Of course, truly health-conscious Japanese may shun social convention altogether and simply refuse all forms of liquor. Such nonconformists have the option of guzzling popular non-alcoholic beverages such as Pocari Sweat, Calpis Water, Fanta Muscat, and Mucos. Now these are names that would drive anyone to drink.

Song of the Salaryman

KARAOKE

sing-along

Before your next business trip to Japan, consider brushing up on vocal renditions of "My Way," "Feelings," "Que Será, Será," and "Raindrops Keep Fallin' On My Head." These syrupy ditties are sure to come in handy when your Japanese associates cajole you into participating in *karaoke*, the infectiously fun practice of singing into a microphone accompanied by background music. Already flourishing in hundreds of thousands of Japanese bars and restaurants and millions of homes, karaoke continues to make its way throughout Japan and beyond.

Karaoke literally means "empty orchestra" (*kara* is "empty" and *oke* is short for "orchestra"). Electronic karaoke was spawned in the early 1970s as a simple combination of microphone and cassette player, but soon electronics companies successfully cross-fertilized sound and video technology and brought to market a new breed: laser disc karaoke. It combines a laser disc that projects videos with a souped-up sound system that blends any voice into a smooth, Sinatra-esque flow. Reinforced by digital sound, echo effects, and slick videos replete with lyrics and a bouncing ball, any amateur can revel in a few minutes of E-Z listening fame.

As karaoke's popularity in Japan reached symphonic proportions, it took firm root in corporate culture. After a long day at the office, groups of co-workers, bosses, and their clients head for karaoke bars such as The You and I Communication Space, Art Sound, and Voice Bank. After a few drinks, each person takes a turn crooning into the mike, thus experiencing a uniquely Japanese form of off-key bonding. This routine is so widespread that books on corporate etiquette counsel young salarymen to practice their singing, and night schools throughout the land are available to train the timid. Lesson number one: never sing the boss's song.

A book published by a Japanese government agency advises foreigners doing business in Japan that few things impress a Japanese businessman more than a foreigner who can belt out karaoke songs in Japanese. To this end, several language schools now offer intensive karaoke training in English.

Those who cannot afford the high prices of the karaoke club can enjoy the pastime in an ever-increasing range of settings. There are home versions of karaoke (which may not endear you to the family upstairs) and karaoke-equipped tour buses and taxis which provide musical entertainment to a more or less captive audience. Recently, so-called karaoke boxes such as The Melon have also struck a chord with the Japanese. These soundproof cubicles are miniature music studios with stylish sofas and deluxe laser karaoke. For the upscale singer, Tokyo's

Big Echo offers thirty-seven karaoke boxes in a four-story building luxuriously layered with marble floors.

Karaoke is popular outside Japan, too. Many Koreans love it, although the Korean government, recalling bitter memories of the Japanese occupation, tried to slow its growth by officially outlawing the sale of Japanese songs. In Memphis, Tennessee, across the street from Elvis Presley's mansion, fans can now record their own versions of Elvis's songs on karaoke, courtesy of the Songmasters' Graceland Recording Studio & Singalong Shop. Elsewhere in America, outbreaks of karaoke have occurred at weddings, bar mitzvahs, parties, and country clubs. Despite pockets of enthusiasm in the United States, overall lackluster sales of karaoke machines suggest that the fad is not likely to crescendo anytime soon in America.

Even in Japan, karaoke is not an unmitigated success. In Tokyo, kill-joy complaints equating karaoke with noise pollution led to laws limiting the hours and volume of karaoke. And musicians' groups have made claims against karaoke bars for the unauthorized use of their tunes in karaoke background music. Nevertheless, as long as karaoke crooners remain determined to turn a deaf ear to such complaints, chagrined musicians and unsympathetic listeners will just have to do their best to tune out the warbling of amateurs.

III

the
TRADITIONAL
WORLD

Back in the Heart of Old Edo

SHITAMACHI

old town

Beyond the wafting incense and flocks of pigeons, through the throngs of tourists and down a lane of shops outside the Kannon temple in Asakusa, sits a small, hundred-year-old family business selling cosmetics. Inside is the last place in Tokyo that sells the precious skin cleanser composed of powdered bird droppings that geisha, generations ago, loved to daub on their faces. In the downtown areas of Tokyo, called *shitamachi*, the ambience of old Edo—Tokyo's former name—still lingers. Although currently threatened by new development, these neighborhoods of narrow streets, temples, and wooden houses are still encrusted with an urban culture and charm hundreds of years old. They are the heart of old Tokyo, where commoners traditionally lived and plied their trades, and where kabuki, geisha, and sumo first thrived.

Literally meaning "the town below," the word shitamachi derives from the ancient shogun's practice of forcing the lower classes of society, especially the merchants and artisans, to occupy the marshy lands

below his castle. While the upper crust quietly enjoyed the somber ambience of Noh theater, tradesmen down in the lowlands hooted and cheered for their favorite actors—including female impersonators—in shitamachi kabuki theaters. As the ruling class of samurai practiced their swordsmanship and other military arts forbidden to the commoners, the shitamachi inhabitants gawked at the clash of fleshy titans in the sumo rings. And while the elite ladies refined their poetry and music, shitamachi spawned pleasure quarters such as Yoshiwara. These vibrant worlds of kabuki, sumo, and the pleasure quarters have been captured for posterity in the bright colors and bold designs of woodblock prints.

The flavor of shitamachi pervades the district of Asakusa, where one of Tokyo's most famous temples, Sensoji, is crowned with two towering red lanterns—the biggest in the city—like brash beacons of shitamachi character. Surrounding the temple are small, timeless shops which have remained in the same place and family for generations. They sell everything from seaweed shampoo and blowfish-shaped paper kites to the mind-boggling array of combs and brushes needed to groom a geisha's intricately designed hair. On festival days, the Asakusa temple grounds burst with visitors in colorful kimono, toy merchants, performers, mendicants, and soothsayers. The scene seems unchanged from decades ago—well, almost unchanged, since palm readers today sometimes resort to computers in order to deliver speedier fortunes.

Another area that is vibrant with shitamachi character is Ueno, which draws up to one million people a day, especially during cherry blossom season when Ueno Park is ablaze with petals. Near the park is an outdoor shopping area bustling with shrewd shoppers and savvy merchants aggressively pitching their wares. Boasting the lowest prices in Tokyo, the market contrasts sharply with the chic, coolly elegant department stores of the Ginza. Ueno is also home to the Shitamachi Museum, which houses reconstructions of a typical turn-of-the-century public bath, home, and candy store. In keeping with the neighborly spirit of shitamachi, the downtown residents donated the commemorative museum objects, which visitors are encouraged to handle.

The twentieth century has not been kind to shitamachi. The Great Kanto Earthquake ripped through the old neighborhoods and set off raging fires that destroyed the narrow streets and tightly packed wooden structures. Even more devastating, World War II firebombing obliterated whole neighborhoods. Today, the forces of modernization slowly encroach upon the surviving shitamachi areas.

With the fierce pride of shitamachi, many local residents are resisting the destruction of their neighborhoods. When the owners of a generations-old fabric-dying company were compelled for environmental reasons to move their old factory, they reportedly received several lucrative offers from developers eager to exploit the location. The company moved but did not sell out, choosing instead to convert the real estate into an arts center where actors and directors today rehearse experimental plays. In another effort to preserve shitamachi, downtown Tokyo residents created a magazine devoted to the arts and ways of the neighborhood that carries articles about local life, interviews with old-world shop owners, and surveys of the best public baths.

Even though trendy areas such as Harajuku, Shinjuku, and Roppongi have today overtaken districts such as Asakusa and Ueno as the capital's main commercial and entertainment centers, the spirit of shitamachi is still very much alive. As you begin to lose yourself in the crowds and incense of Asakusa's Kannon temple, it is not difficult to imagine the time not long ago when such areas were mere marshes and to feel that you are back in the heart of old Edo.

A Horticultural Snow Flurry

HANAMI

cherry blossom viewing

Spring is a stressful time for Japanese weather forecasters, who each year must predict exactly when the national flower—the cherished cherry blossom, or *sakura*—will bloom. As meteorologists feverishly track the northerly spread of the so-called cherry blossom front, Japanese everywhere eagerly make plans to revel in *hanami*, meaning "cherry blossom viewing."

The moment Japan's stunning pink petals burst onto the scene, loyal cherry blossom fans abandon their desks, schools, and homes and head for the nearest cherry-tree parks. There, they kick off their shoes, settle onto tatami mats or picnic blankets under boughs heavy with flowers, and indulge in exuberant merrymaking and lots and lots of saké. For purists, it's a time to feast one's eyes on the blossoms, pose in silken kimono, and scribble poetic reveries inspired by the fragile flowers. For businesses, it's the moment when one junior associate is allowed to leave work early to stake out a choice spot under the trees for his or her

colleagues who will follow later. And for many others, it's simply a good excuse to break out the microphones and amplifiers for rounds of animated *karaoke* singing that will last well into the night.

During one recent cherry blossom fest at Tokyo's Ueno Park, the high-spirited carousing became so vocal that officials at the adjoining zoo finally complained that the noise was keeping the animals up way past their bedtimes. While all the boisterous fun goes on below the branches, the pale pink blossoms above the crowds create a horticultural snow flurry. Ephemeral petals take over the air, drifting into the laps and cups of the revelers.

The real magic of Japan's cherry blossoms is that they are intense while they last and then gone before you know it. After just a few days of arboreal glory, a simple spring breeze or rainfall reduces the blaze of blossoms to a carpet of scattered petals. Enthralled by the impermanence of the flowers, Japanese poets have romantically likened them to the transience of beauty, love, and life itself. In Japanese folklore and literature, the fleeting cherry blossoms have even come to symbolize the samurai, those ideal warriors whose noble lives were often cut short by ritual suicides.

In 1912, the mayor of Tokyo decided to spread around the enchanting blossoms by presenting Washington, D.C., with 3,000 cherry-tree saplings as a "memorial of national friendship between the U.S. and Japan." In 1988, the Japan Cherry Blossom Association also did its part to break the ice in international relations by giving the state of Alaska 5,000 seeds of a strain of cherry tree that is especially resistant to very cold weather.

So great is the cherry blossom's appeal that the country's second-largest bank, Mitsui Taiyo Kobe, even decided to change its name to Sakura Bank, meaning "Cherry Blossom Bank." While the bank's new name and the tellers' spiffy cherry-colored uniforms and pink pens admittedly add a certain aesthetic appeal, depositors might feel a trifle nervous entrusting their hard-earned funds to a bank named after a flower that blooms so briefly . . . and then quickly disappears.

Just a Peek at the Peak

FUJI-SAN

Mount Fuji

For those wanting to steep themselves in a higher understanding of Japanese culture, a lofty beginning is Japan's top mountain, Fuji-san, otherwise known as Mount Fuji. Seen from a distance, the snowcapped cone rising above the clouds and reflected in Lake Yamanaka below is awesome and uplifting. Actually climbing the majestic mountain, however, can be more of a rocky, downhill experience.

Fuji-san is a Japanese icon. Artists have memorialized its symmetrical silhouette in dramatic woodblock prints, alluded to it in symbolic rock gardens, and splashed it on postcards. Some have suggested moving the country's capital to the foot of the sacred mountain. Others are yearning to be buried at Fuji's base, a coveted grave site. Resort hotels which look out onto Mount Fuji provide the ultimate rooms with a view— one inn even reportedly offers refunds if the mountain is not visible from a guest's room for at least sixty seconds. Admiring the vista from a slightly higher vantage point,

the first Japanese in orbit enthusiastically pointed out Fuji to his earthbound audience.

Each year, hundreds of thousands of eager visitors from around the world straggle up the 12,390-foot high mountain. Hulda Crooks made the pilgrimage when she was ninety-five. The much younger Ashrita Furman climbed only one-third of the mountain—but then again he was on a pogo stick at the time. In the summer, when Fuji is less snowy and cloudy, climbers set out in the early morning for the nine-hour trek up one of the five paths, stopping occasionally at stations for food, shelter, and rest. For the full effect, some climb all night, or sleep at a mountain hut and rise before dawn, to greet the sunrise over Fuji with cheers of *"Banzai!"*

Part of the ascent's down side is that the trails are crowded with tourists (Tokyo is, after all, only two hours away), the volcanic rock is slippery, and the actual hike can be aesthetically lacking. The paths are lined with soda machines and souvenir shops selling . . . what else but . . . Fuji film. Furthermore, since Mount Fuji is actually a dormant volcano which last erupted in 1707 but which may have recently reentered an active phase, a stroll up the mountain can end with a bang. According to one Japanese saying, only a fool climbs Fuji twice.

Many visitors to Japan are exposed to Fuji-san for only a few brief moments as they whiz by in the bullet train. Taking in the mountain this way—in a flash of shape and color—may, in fact, be the most memorable way to experience it. After all, to some purists, the aesthetic experience peaks when you take just a peek at the peak.

The Killer Whale, the Temple Gong, and the Sea Slug

SUMOO

sumo wrestling

The two near-naked fatties enter the sandbox, throw salt into the air, make faces at each other, squat, stomp their feet, slap their buttocks, and then charge—pushing, shoving, and grappling each other—until one tumbles over. The scene may sound like recess at a local kindergarten or a mating ritual for elephants, but the combatants are actually four-hundred-pound *rikishi*, or wrestlers, dressed in skimpy silk loincloths and engaged in Japan's most revered sport, sumo wrestling.

The object of sumo is to force one's opponent out of the *dohyoo*—a fifteen-foot-diameter ring made of sand and clay—or to make him touch the dohyoo with any part of his body other than his feet. Although a typical bout lasts less than a minute and seems childishly simple, it is actually surprisingly complex. For instance, during the period of *niramiai*, or "war of nerves," each wrestler tries to unhinge the other by eyeballing him

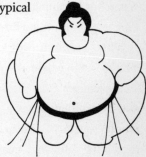

menacingly. Moreover, ambitious wrestlers may attempt to master up to seventy different sumo maneuvers, all of which require amazing displays of raw strength and weight-balancing. Undeterred by the sport's lack of weight classifications, a really agile athlete can, with a bit of fancy footwork, dispose of a far heftier opponent in seconds. And since kicking, punching, and scratching are considered foul play, sumo is relatively safe.

According to legend, the Japanese islands were originally won in a sumo match between two gods, and to this day the sport is still steeped in history, religion, and ritual. Before each tournament, a referee cloaked in the white robes of a Shinto priest purifies the sacred dohyoo, which is crowned with a tasseled roof similar to the type found in Shinto shrines. A senior referee also bears a dagger, since traditionally he is supposed to pay for an incorrect ruling with his life (modern-day referees tend to skip this messy custom). Upon entering the ring, each wrestler appeases the gods by clapping (a solemn act usually done before Shinto shrines) and casting great handfuls of salt into the air. He then lifts his legs sideways and stomps his feet thunderously to drive away unfriendly spirits.

Most wrestlers join so-called sumo stables. These are rigidly hierarchical training camps where underling athletes literally wipe the sweat off the brows of their superiors, where insubordination results in corporal punishment from the "stablemaster," and where even in cold weather only sissies wear socks. Athletes eat a mere two meals a day, but they compensate by wolfing down a daily average of fifty-five thousand calories worth of *chanko nabe*, a special stew cooked in vats containing industrial quantities of meat, fish, seaweed, eggs, vegetables, and tofu. This non-dietetic delicacy is washed down with equally healthy portions of rice and beer (wrestlers watching their figures can skip dessert).

Bearing such apt English nicknames as "Killer Whale," "Temple Gong," and "Sea Slug," each wrestler wears his shiny black hair in an eighteenth-century-style topknot which is glued together with aromatic grease. At the athlete's retirement ceremony, tradition demands that the knot be lopped off, Samson-style, in the presence of the sumo elders.

Precisely because sumo is so uniquely Japanese, foreign wrestlers have a tough time advancing in the sport. The Japan Sumo Association reportedly still bars foreigners from opening a sumo stable. And until recently, the prospect of a non-Japanese bearing the coveted title *yokozuna*, or grand champion (who is viewed as both a helper of Shinto spirits and a modern-day samurai), was inconceivable to many traditional-minded Japanese. But in 1993 the soft-spoken former Hawaiian basketball player Chad Rowan went down in sumo history as the first foreigner to be named a grand champion. Known as "The Dawn," Chad out-swiped his opponents inside the ring and proved himself outside the ring by exhibiting the quiet dignity that is considered fitting for a true sumo star.

Chad Rowan may have paved the way for foreigners, but women are still excluded from sumo competition on the theory that they will defile the sacrosanct ring if they get too close. In fact, when Japan's Chief Cabinet Secretary publicly announced her intention to enter the ring to present a trophy to a sumo champion, she was politely but firmly reminded that the ring is off limits to her sex. She eventually relented.

Whether or not one appreciates sumo's conservative side, watching the Olympian sport can still be addictively suspenseful and gratifying, especially for couch-potato spectators who themselves enjoy the occasional tub of pistachio ice cream. Some Japanese women also claim that sumo can be a profoundly erotic sport, although don't ask why. If nothing else, each match creates the thrilling possibility that one of the quarter-ton behemoths will be flung from the ring and land on an unsuspecting onlooker, or—even more alarming—that the brute's skimpy loincloth will break off and all hell will break loose.

A Few Good Tattooed Men

YAKUZA

gangsters

Next time you run into a tattooed Japanese fellow with a tight perm, gold teeth, and only nine fingers, it might be best to walk the other way. Chances are, he is a *yakuza*, or Japanese gangster.

Yakuza are reputed to traffic in drugs and pornography, manage international prostitution and gambling rings, and engage in loan-sharking and racketeering. Typically, they harass debtors, extort protection money from businessmen, or act as *sookaiya*, who blackmail companies by threatening to disrupt shareholder meetings.

Japanese gangsters have become firmly established as a tolerated, if not entirely accepted, part of Japanese tradition. Yakuza ceremonies are viewed as time-honored, mystical rituals which, even if private, are very much a part of public lore. For instance, during one yakuza initiation ceremony held in a rough quarter of Tokyo, local police reportedly took the trouble of cordoning off adjacent sidewalks to prevent curious onlookers from interfering with the proceedings. At the same time, the yakuza present at the ceremony

125

donned traditional black kimono and surrounded their new leader in a rite that included homage to the patron god of warriors.

The very name *yakuza*—which applies to individual members as well as to the organization itself—is hundreds of years old. The word means "good-for-nothing" and is derived from a card game similar to blackjack in which the object was to draw three cards that approach but do not exceed a total of nineteen. Ya-ku-za specifically refers to "eight," "nine," and "three," a worthless score.

Yakuza also claim to live by an ancient code of honor which requires that a yakuza who bungles a job must atone by taking knife in hand and cutting off one-third of his finger. Truly incompetent yakuza have been known to have difficulty mustering enough fingers to balance their rice bowls. Because of this digital deformation, former yakuza have traditionally had a hard time easing back into normal society. Today, however, a new operation that grafts a toe (or toes) onto fingers has successfully allowed former gangsters to turn over a new leaf.

A new yakuza initiate is likely to be an *ochikobore*, or "a person who has fallen between the cracks," and is often recruited from motorcycle gangs. While a low-level yakuza may be easily recognizable by the tattoos peeking out from under his polo shirt, his heavy gold jewelry, and white shoes—a manner of dress similar to that of a vacationing American used-car salesman—his higher-ranking colleague will often be indistinguishable from an ordinary businessman.

For the moment, Japanese still disagree about whether

yakuza are friends or foes, guardians or gangsters. On the one hand, membership in yakuza groups is not illegal. Japanese police routinely leave the yakuza alone, and when a serious crime occurs, law officers expect the yakuza to hand over both the culprit and weapon within a few days. On the other hand, this leniency is slowly disappearing; recently, the Japanese parliament passed legislation designed to combat organized crime.

To be safe, you might want to give your neighborhood yakuza wide berth. Think of him as somewhere between, say, Robin Hood and Al Capone.

Less Than a Golden Opportunity

ROOJIN

senior citizens

Like geriatric heaven, Japan has traditionally venerated *roojin*, or "old people." Many members of the country's so-called "silver society," meaning Japanese senior citizens, live in protective, extended families and bask in the safety and orderliness of supportive communities. With so much going for the elderly, it's hard to believe that, a few years back, the Japanese government reportedly cooked up a controversial plan to deal with some of its senior citizens: ship them out of the country.

The Ministry of International Trade and Industry designed the "Silver Columbia Plan" in 1987 to create overseas Japanese retirement colonies by 1992 (five hundred years after Columbus's arrival in America) in the United States, Mexico, Spain, and other sunny locations. The plan was intended in part to ease Japan's old-age burden: with a plunging birthrate, Japan has the world's fastest-aging population, and its citizens now enjoy the longest average lifespan (seventy-six for men and

eighty-two for women). Although the plan died a natural death because an incensed public viewed it as a form of "granny-dumping," it vividly demonstrates how severe Japan's old age crunch has become.

Before World War II the eldest son inherited all his family's land and provided for his parents, but the postwar change to equal inheritance worked against such filial piety. Moreover, today, as young couples move from the country to the city, they are finding that staggering real estate costs and space constraints make housing an aged mom or pop much tougher. To complicate matters, as wives begin to leave their houses to work, no one is around to tend to a frail, live-in in-law. Since nursing homes are scarce, old people increasingly seek refuge in overcrowded hospitals that are ill-equipped to look after them but that, thanks to the national health insurance program, at least offer low-cost care.

On the brighter side, many more older Japanese live in extended families than in, say, the United States. Moreover, Japan actively celebrates its senior citizens. On the national holiday, respect for the Aged Day, the Japanese public honors those who have reached 100—and even presents them with silver cups bearing the name of the prime minister. The government is also doing its part to keep senior citizens productive by, for example, raising the retirement age and establishing a Silver Personnel Center which finds part-time employment for the over-sixty set. Similarly, the private Japan Well-Aging Association creates volunteer positions for seniors. The commercial sector is also waking up to the graying of Japan and targeting so-called woopies—well-off older people. Businesses are planning retirement communities, old-age parks, automated homes, adjustable beds, house-cleaning and bathing services, travel programs, and health care consulting. As a result, the "silver market" is estimated to reach $700 billion by the end of the century.

Nourished on a healthy, high-fiber, low-fat diet of fish, vegetables, rice, and very little beef, the Japanese now have the chance to enjoy longer and fuller lives than ever before. At the same time, however, the golden years may be less than a golden opportunity for idle retirees who are sometimes jokingly dismissed as *sodai gomi*, or "unwieldy refuse." All this goes to show that getting old in Japan just isn't what it used to be.

Things Are Seldom What They Seem

HONNE/TATEMAE

reality/appearance

Ask your sushi chef for some ketchup and he's liable to clench his teeth, nervously suck in a deep breath of air, and sputter, "Yes, well, that could be just a little bit difficult." What the chef would really be thinking, of course, is: "Sushi with ketchup? Over my dead body! Get lost!" In Japan, one's true feelings, or *honne*, are often sugar-coated with an idealized facade, or *tatemae*.

Like an attractive mask presented to the outside world, tatemae blurs the unpalatable truth and thus allows the speaker to avoid disappointing the listener and losing face in the process. When your Japanese engineer casually remarks with a smile, "I wonder if this structure was built with the correct specifications," chances are this is tatemae and the real meaning, or honne, is: "Run for the hills! The building's coming down!" Similarly, an initial round of business negotiations with potential Japanese partners might produce lots of noncommittal smiling and nodding, but after investing some time in getting to know them (which may include after-hours entertainment), you'll find them more likely to open up and reveal their real intent unambiguously. Dropping tatemae takes time.

Politicians in Japan, as most everywhere else perhaps, can be masters of tatemae, yet a number of Japan's most skilled statesmen have inadvertently let the mask slip. When Prime Minister Miyazawa said that Americans "may have lacked a work ethic" and later explained that he had not intended to criticize American workers, was this an example of honne followed by tatemae backpedaling? How about when the speaker of Japan's lower house of parliament attributed the trade deficit to "inferior American workers" and later explained that he had merely intended to call for an improvement in the quality of the American work force? Or when Prime Minister Nakasone made a seemingly disparaging comment about American minorities and later apologized to the U.S. Congress?

In nonconfrontational Japan, candor is often sacrificed for the sake of group harmony, and things are seldom what they seem. If honne is the truth, is tatemae a white lie? A polite way of waffling? Or simply a form of tact that any Japanese would recognize as such? Many Japanese scholars still disagree on these questions—and will suck in air nervously when asked for a straight answer.

Stiff Upper Lip

GAMAN

perseverance

Virtuous Japanese keep their heads to the grindstone, their noses in their schoolbooks, and their eyes on the ball, while at the same time gritting their teeth and maintaining stiff upper lips. Such facial contortions may seem strenuous and painful, but that's the idea behind the Japanese virtue *gaman*, loosely translated as "perseverance."

Company workers reveal gaman when commuting on overcrowded subways and slogging away at the same company for years. Foreign companies that are continually unsuccessful in breaking into the Japanese market have been faulted for lacking in gaman. Housewives exhibit the virtue when waiting silently in tiny apartments for overworked husbands to drag themselves home. Ex-president Bush's wife Barbara got high marks for gaman when she sat by stoically as her husband threw up over the Japanese prime minister at a state dinner.

Other paragons of gaman include survivors of a postwar impoverished Japan who determinedly rebuilt the country; sumo wrestlers who doggedly fight for top honors; company shareholders who forego handsome dividends for the sake of long-term corporate results; and even participants in sadomasochistic Japanese television game shows, such as the one that requires Velcro-clad contestants to hurl themselves against a Velcro-padded wall to see if they can stick.

To some outside critics, many Japanese tend to overdo gaman and make their lives unnecessarily harsh. From the Japanese perspective, however, human experience is a mix of both sweet and sour, and those who are unable or unwilling to pepper their days with stamina, perseverance, and a "fighting spirit" are the ones missing out on the true spice of life.

In traditional Japan, "real men" know how to gaman, and those who can't are, quite simply, wimps.

Chances Are You Have Done Something Wrong

AYAMARU

apologize

"Dear Pen-Pal: My profoundest apologies for my hesitating to send you a letter. Whenever I face to the typewriter, deep sigh rushed me to conquer. I wondered how to express my emotion and thought by my hopeless English. This is my excuse for delaying. I am afraid of you to be disappointed at my silence. It will be most generous of you to forgive me. . . ." As this letter from Japan suggests, the Japanese like to *ayamaru*, or apologize. A lot.

To maintain the illusion of harmony and to avoid ruffling feathers, Japanese often litter their speech with expressions of remorse, such as the refrains *sumimasen* and *gomen nasai* ("I'm sorry.") A routine telephone conversation can sound like a duet of don't-mention-it's, with each speaker vying to out-pardon the other: "It was rude of me not to call earlier" . . . "No, I'm terribly sorry for having been out of touch" . . . "But how inexcusable of me to take up your valuable time" . . . "Not at all, it is I who have been indiscreet in disturbing

you" . . . "Now please forgive my hanging up the receiver. . . ."

In all aspects of Japanese life, there's no excuse for not saying you're sorry. For instance, in reaction to a Japan Airlines plane crash, the airline's president wrote personal condolence letters to the victims' families, apologized "from the bottom of our hearts," and resigned in shame. When brokerage firms were caught making improper payments to clients, company heads said they felt really terrible about the situation and the finance minister took a pay cut. At the Olympics, famed figure skater Midori Ito formally apologized to all of Japan for missing a jump which caused her to forfeit the gold medal and settle for second place.

Strangely enough, one of the few times that Japanese seem to dry their tears and dispense with their apologies is in crowds. Squeezed together in an overstuffed bus, a passenger could be squashed by a careless sumo wrestler or skewered by an old lady's umbrella while hearing not a peep from the offender. In most other situations, it's good form to bow and scrape, even if you're not sure what you've done wrong. (Chances are you have done *something* wrong—you just don't know what.) Legalistic Westerners shouldn't worry that such groveling will be misinterpreted as a confession of liability. In a triumph of form over substance, penitence in Japan needn't be genuine and isn't necessarily an admission of guilt—especially if it is artfully phrased in the passive voice.

Is it a regrettable oversimplification to say that Japanese are constantly contrite? If so, apologies are in order. *Mea culpa.*

It's Not Just the Thought That Counts

OKURIMONO

gifts

Next time you reach into your Christmas stocking, how would you like to find a bottle of blowfish-flavored saké? A solid gold ear-swab? Or a year's supply of vegetable oil? These are just some of the *okurimono* (gifts) that abound in Japan, a land that has become completely wrapped up in frenzied gift-giving.

The Japanese lavish presents on each other on every conceivable occasion: before an operation, from a patient to his or her surgeon; after a wedding, from the newlyweds to their guests; at a funeral, from mourners to the nearest and dearest, and even vice versa. Such offerings are prompted by the feudal concept of *giri*, or obligation, and the sense that, in a highly interdependent society, debts to others must be paid off—literally.

Exchanging gifts climaxes twice a year, during *ochuugen* ("mid-year") in July, and the more important *oseibo* ("year-end") in December. Oseibo coincides conveniently with year-end bonus time, when company employees customarily receive an extra

two or three months' pay. On these occasions, presents are given by social and economic underlings to their superiors, whether by employees to their bosses or tenants to their land-lords. As long as the offering hails from a prestigious depart-ment store and is properly wrapped and priced, it needn't be thrilling or even bear any relationship to the recipient. Popular oseibo and ochuugen items include instant coffee, towels, green tea, and that handy standby, gift-pack laundry soap.

Ecologically-oriented gifts range from canned oxygen to a beverage called "Earth Beer" (unfortunately, the can is non-recyclable). Practical-minded Japanese sometimes prefer to give gift certificates rather than the real thing. This not only comes as a relief to recipients who simply don't have room for another case of dried seaweed or another bottle of oxygen, but it has also led to a thriving resale market for discount brokers. Some shops now purchase department store certificates at six to eight percent below the listed price.

On Japanese Valentine's Day, a Western import also cele-brated on February 14, the most popular gift is chocolate, and the happy rule for men is that women give and men receive. Valentine's chocolates are either *rabu choko* ("love chocolate") for a boyfriend, *doojoo choko* ("sympathy chocolate") for men who don't qualify for rabu choko, or *giri choko* ("obligation chocolate") for those employers, teachers, and others who have rendered favors. Men get a chance to reciprocate on White Day (March 14) when they offer women white-colored sweets sym-bolizing purity. Traditional White Day presents include white chocolate (a sign of true love) or, for the more loosely defined relationship, marshmallows.

All self-respecting Japanese vacationers returning home must arm themselves with *omiyage* (souvenirs) such as silver key chains from Tiffany's or anything else with a brand-name label. The pressure to bring back omiyage has become so fierce that, for Japanese coming back to Japan empty-handed, some Tokyo airport shops now sell gifts which are specially wrapped to look as though they were acquired abroad. One such store is well stocked with "Discovery of Singapore Chocolates," "Thailand Macadamia Nuts," "Hawaii's Beef Steak Jerky," and "Trebor Traditional English Sweets."

Exchanging gifts is so rampant in Japanese business and political circles that it has begun to blur the line between mere tokens of good will and outright bribes. A few years ago, insider stock tip "gifts" to politicians played a key role in the so-called Recruit Scandal which tainted influential businessmen and government officials and even toppled a prime minister or two.

When making offerings in Japan, it is best to follow the rules. The right way to give a present is to bow slightly, extend the gift with both hands, and murmur sheepishly, "It's really a boring item" (which, in the case of vegetable oil, may even have the ring of truth). When accepting a present, first hesitate so as not to appear too greedy, and open it only later, once the donor is out of sight. Unless you are heading off to a friend's wake, avoid giving presents which symbolize death or are associated with funerals, such as packages in black-and-white wrapping paper or cash gifts with the numeral "four" (the word for "four" in Japanese sounds like "death"). Finally, steer clear of presents which depict a sixteen-petal chrysanthemum (the royal family has exclusive dibs on this imperial crest symbol), a badger (the symbol for scavenger), or a fox (the symbol for cunning).

Foreigners unschooled in Asian etiquette should do some homework to avoid presenting the wrong gift. A cautionary tale is the case of one of New York City's former mayors who, after accepting a sizable charitable donation from a prominent Japanese executive, reportedly reciprocated by handing the fellow a polyester "Big Apple" necktie. The mayor apparently failed to realize that in Japan it's not just the thought that counts.

Shake and Bake

JISHIN

earthquake

Aforeign newcomer to Tokyo was chatting with her Japanese roommate when she suddenly felt an express train rush past the apartment. After the windows stopped shaking, she remarked: "I didn't realize the tracks were so close." "What tracks?" asked her friend nonchalantly. "That was just a jishin—an earthquake." When Japan is hit by a minor *jishin*, jaded Japanese often remain calm, while others are rocked with that gnawing question: "To quake or not to quake?"

Home to one-tenth of the world's strongest earthquakes, Japan regularly experiences small tremors and is beset by a major quake every sixty years or so. In 1995, an earthquake devastated the unsuspecting residents of Kobe, killing 5,000 and leaving 300,000 homeless. It was Japan's worst natural disaster since 1923, when the Great Kanto Quake levelled Tokyo. Striking at around midday, that earthquake toppled stoves that had been lit for lunchtime and led to an outbreak of fires that quickly consumed wooden residences. It demolished

580,000 buildings and left more than 140,000 dead.

Tokyo is unusually prone to earthquakes because three plates of the earth's crust collide below it. Moreover, some Tokyo homes stand on land that was reclaimed from Tokyo Bay and that could sink right into mud at a jolt from the earth. In light of the city's precarious footing, why was the country's capital moved there from the more geologically stable Kyoto in 1869? This is a sensitive question that may induce officials to experience nervous tremors while dodging the issue of personal and geological fault.

Today, Japan's federal government spends billions of dollars annually on earthquake research and damage prevention. Wooden buildings must meet strict height limitations and apartment complexes are often constructed with concrete and steel engineered to withstand vibrations. Skyscrapers are sometimes equipped with seismic shock absorbers—the equivalent of rubber legs. Increasingly, homes are built to sway rather than crumble and use gas lines that shut off automatically at the first sign of trouble. Some bridges have vibration-dampening systems, and today's Japanese structures are now routinely tested for resistance to tremors and fires—a strict scrutiny that one foreign observer dubbed the "shake and bake" test.

Every September 1, the anniversary of the devastating Great Kanto Quake, is Disaster Prevention Day. Japanese mark the occasion by partaking in elaborate earthquake drills that include evacuating to emergency sites and readying earthquake kits that contain flashlights, food, and water. When a real quake hits, the Japanese know to crawl under a sturdy desk or table, away from falling debris; outside, open parks are considered a safe bet. Should a major quake strike, a council made up of six seismological sages will convene in a Tokyo bunker to evaluate the situation and decide whether and when to notify the prime minister, who may alert the rest of the country.

Although experts still cannot predict earthquakes with any certainty, some animals are said to emit warning signs and behave strangely before a quake hits. For instance, there have been prequake reports of alligators crying, chickens climbing trees, bears going bonkers, and normally docile catfish acting uppity. So remember: if your crocodile gets cranky, your hen gets high, your bear becomes unbearable, and your fish starts fidgeting, it's time to size up the seismological situation. Run for cover! You're in the wake of a quake!

Of Ghosts and Men

KAIDAN

ghost stories

In love with his wealthy neighbor's granddaughter and devoid of all feeling for his wife, Iyemon plots murder. Through gradual poisoning, he does away with his wife, Oiwa, but only after the "medicine" disfigures her beauty and causes her to writhe in agony. In the end, the hideous ghost of Oiwa—partially bald, one eye swollen, and the other turned up into her head—returns to seek revenge. . . .

Send chills down your spine? That's the idea behind Japanese *kaidan*, or ghost stories, which abound in Japanese theater, literature, folklore, and art and make for wickedly delightful entertainment. Judging from the number of supernatural stories and legends, Japan must be one of the most haunted lands on earth. Its literature and art crawl with strange creatures and otherworldly apparitions conjured up from a brew of Buddhist, Shinto, and folk beliefs. The eerie figures range from magical animals and goblins such as oversized toads, snakes, foxes, and flesh-eating demons to *yuurei*—the vengeful souls of the deceased— such as dead lovers, warriors, and even emperors.

Well-known among ghost groupies are *tengu*, or mountain goblins. Armed with pointy beaks and wings, they mischievously scoop up priests during meditations and tie them to the tops of tall trees and towers. Tengu are also blamed for throwing pebbles into houses at night, setting fire to Buddhist temples, and whisking away small children only to return them in a stupor. In the countryside today, some superstitious locals will not cut down trees until they have made offerings of cakes and sweets to the tengu in the area.

The *kappa*, or water imp, another ghostly favorite, looks something like a turtle. On its head it balances a saucer full of water that, if spilled, will cause the creature to die of thirst. Magical foxes also abound in Japan. They sometimes take the form of women in order to trick unsuspecting victims into marriage.

From Buddhist mythology arise tales of fearsome *oni*, or demons. With bulging eyes, wide grins crammed with jagged teeth, and claws for fingers and toes, oni also cause nasty surprises. According to one tale, a tenth-century hero offered a beautiful maiden a ride on his horse only to have her transform herself into a hideous oni. The warrior managed to lop off the demon's arm just as it reached forward to pluck off his head. The triumphant fellow kept the arm safely locked up in a chest until one day the oni returned, disguised as the man's aunt. Changing back to its demonic form, the oni snatched back the arm and fled.

With so many beasties on the loose, it is lucky that Japan is protected by a formidable ghost-buster: Shoki the Demon Queller. After failing the civil entrance exam and committing suicide in shame, the Demon Queller was nonetheless given a dignified government funeral. To repay the kindness, he promised in afterlife to hunt down demons as a sort of public service. Beginning his ghost-busting career in seventh-century China, he became known in Japan as a fearsome, towering, bearded figure with blazing eyes who gathers up ghoulish creatures, sometimes enthusiastically poking out their eyes and gobbling the goblins whole.

According to beliefs rooted in Buddhism and folk religion, those who die violently or in the grip of a powerful emotion remain trapped in limbo and haunt a place or person until released from their final predicaments. For example, in the case of the servant girl Okiku, her master hid one of the household's ten treasured plates and then falsely accused her of losing the plate. When he promised to forgive all if she married him and she refused, he murdered her in a blind rage and threw her body into a well. From then on, Okiku's pitiful ghost could be seen by the well counting plates, always breaking into a long, piercing wail before reaching number ten. One night, the ghost was finally exorcised by a clever priest who, waiting until the apparition had counted up to number nine, jumped out from behind the well and yelled, "Ten!"

Ghost stories such as Okiku's are traditionally told on warm summer nights in Japan. Recounted properly, they are guaranteed to cool down the listener with long, icy shivers.

Theater High and Low

Kabuki and Noh

After the dashing warrior Yoemon abandons his lover, Kasane, she catches up to him at a river bank and persuades him to join her in a double suicide. Before taking his life, Yoemon finds a grave marker and a sickle protruding from a skull floating in the river. Amazingly, this was the very same sickle he used to murder his former lover's jealous husband—the man who, coincidentally, was Kasane's father. Suddenly, Yoemon sees Kasane becoming infused with her father's vengeful spirit, and so he raises the sickle and strikes her dead. As Yoemon attempts to flee from the scene of the crime, Kasane's spirit draws him back. . . .

This scene from a nineteenth-century kabuki dance-drama reveals some of the explosive energy conveyed by Japanese kabuki, an offshoot of its austere, fourteenth-century theatrical predecessor, Noh.

Composed of the words *ka* (song), *bu* (dance), and *ki* (skill), kabuki is a flamboyant, stylized spectacle originally intended to entertain merchants, artisans, and other commoners. The plays can be funny, violent, and sensational, treating subjects as diverse as jealousy, drunkenness, and adultery, and dazzling the spectator with characters such as malevolent priests, ghosts, lions, and lovers. Japanese audiences used to pinch evil characters when they ran off the stage, and today's educated spectators still know exactly when to cry out at strategic points throughout the play. At climactic moments, an actor may delight the audience by striking a particularly dramatic fixed pose, rotating his head, and crossing his eyes.

Kabuki performers may change their sumptuous costumes repeatedly in the course of the play. For instance, a character will wear a flat, smooth hairpiece to indicate that he is a sage and then switch to a wig with its hair on end to reveal his anger. The actors also sport brilliantly colorful makeup: crimson lines often denote justice, while blue is associated with evil. The sounds of kabuki instruments can be as vibrant as the colors—there is a haunting three-stringed lute, drums, and a bamboo flute.

Actresses originally performed kabuki but were banned from the stage for engaging in prostitution. Boy actors then took over, but when they too were accused of immoral behavior, they were replaced by adult male actors, who to this day play all the roles. Until recently, Japanese women were advised that they could enhance their own femininity by studying the performance of the men who act out kabuki's female parts.

Kabuki developed in reaction to the more refined Noh drama, a lyrical play that integrates song, speech, music, dance, and mime. Frequently drawing on classical mythology or history, Noh often conveys a tragic theme acted out by spirits, heroes, and priests. A chorus, a small orchestra, and actors dressed in kimono occupy the spare Noh stage, which is built in the form of a shrine and decorated with only a pine tree depicted on the wall. The principal Noh actor, and actors portraying old people or women, wear expressive wooden masks which come in over 150 varieties.

Noh actors chant richly poetic, archaic language laden with symbolism and allusions to ancient verse. As a result, even Japanese audiences may have trouble following the drama, which was intended to be performed strictly for the elite classes. Non-Japanese-speaking audiences don't stand a chance of understanding Noh plays without first reading up on the story. On a lucky day, you may even find English-translation earphones at some Noh theaters.

With little on-stage action or movement, Noh is meticulously slow, subtle, and precise, demanding equal amounts of concentration from the actors and patience from the audience. But at the very least, spectators can relax during the amusing one-act *kyogen* farce, which serves as a comic interlude to a Noh play, or can look forward to lunch-time when the delicious "between the curtains" boxed lunches are available. At its best, Noh seems to distill drama to its essence while radiating an almost mystical intensity—especially when performed on summer nights under the stars on a stage dramatically illuminated by torchlight.

While still played regularly at Tokyo's National Noh Theater, Noh lacks the aristocratic patronage which once supported it and now commands only a limited following. Kabuki audiences have similarly declined, although one controversial kabuki master has helped to revitalize the drama by staging unorthodox interpretations featuring aerial acrobatics, film backdrops, clouds of smoke, and other stunts and special effects. Will Noh and kabuki ever make a complete comeback and draw really large crowds in Japan? For kabuki, with its relatively popular appeal, the answer may be yes. But for the more inaccessible Noh, which was never intended for the masses and which has nevertheless survived hundreds of years, the answer—though closer to no—is harder to know.

Eat Blowfish and Die

FUGU

blowfish

Textured, tough, and toxic, the *fugu*, or Japanese blowfish, is what you might call an acquired taste.

Whether uncooked in the form of *sashimi*, deep-fried in batter as tempura, or dipped in warm saké, the yummy, translucent blowfish is a delicacy in Japan, where a complete meal of fugu averages several hundred dollars. Fugu aficionados swear by the fish's subtle taste, tingling sensation on the tongue, and euphoric, aphrodisiac effects. Never mind that the fish's lethal internal organs, if not properly removed, will constitute the consumer's last meal before he or she succumbs to muscular paralysis and rapid respiratory arrest.

In an effort to cut down on cases of "sushi-cide," fugu chefs are now licensed in Japan and examined on their ability to prepare nondeadly servings of blowfish. Moreover, the U.S. Food and Drug Administration scrutinizes each piece of the glistening fish before it is allowed into America. Even for the fugu experts, however, discerning the deadly from the delicious is deceptively difficult: the blowfish's lethal liver bears an uncanny resemblance to its testicles, a favored dish among *macho* diners who claim that it enhances virility.

Approximately one hundred Japanese fall prey to blowfish poisoning each year. In addition, false alarms occur when a fugu novice mistakes the taste of spicy soy sauce for the onslaught of paralysis, or when a jokester with a sick sense of humor decides to amuse his fellow diners by finishing off a helping of fugu, clutching his throat, and feigning a prolonged finale. The most famous fugu fatality was a kabuki actor who was such a fugu fanatic that he just couldn't resist a nibble of the elusive, lethal liver. Other culinary casualties have included a foolhardy fisherman who devoured his prize catch after a sloppy slicing job, and a pair of daredevil diners who concocted a Russian-roulette stew containing deadly fugu innards. In addition, there are reports of an alleged homicide in Japan involving an unsuspecting diner, a portion of fugu, and a cook with a distinctly fishy alibi.

The gutsy gourmet who is still dead-set on fugu should note that death from ingestion usually occurs after about thirty minutes. Perhaps aware of this grim statistic, one Western establishment that serves blowfish reportedly considered posting a sign outside its window: PAY BEFORE YOU EAT.

A Gripping Challenge

HASHI

chopsticks

"Can you really eat with chopsticks?" Virtually every Western resident of Japan is, at one time or another, subjected to this well-meant but tiresome inquiry. Short-tempered foreigners who are fed up with the question are tempted to reply: "Why yes, thank you . . . and how do you get along with a knife and fork?"

Manipulating chopsticks can be a gripping challenge, especially with paper-thin seaweed, slippery tofu, runny fried eggs, and hard-to-balance beans. Nimble Eastern eaters know how properly to position their chopsticks: one stick resting between the index finger and thumb while the other is held by the middle finger and thumb. Even black belts in Chinese chopstick technique must familiarize themselves with the narrower, lighter, tapered Japanese variety. Another complication is that Japanese chopsticks, like their Chinese forerunners, are made out of varied materials, such as lacquer, wood, ivory, and (in Nara, famous for its deer) even deer antlers. As a rule of thumb, disposable wooden sticks are for eating out, and the reusable, washable kind are customary for home use.

Chopstick protocol is another sticking point when eating with the pointy sticks. Don't lick the chopsticks with your tongue or point with them. When taking food from a serving dish, reach with the clean, unused ends of the utensils. Don't leave the chopsticks upright in a bowl of rice and don't pass food from your chopsticks to another's, since these are funeral rituals. (At a Buddhist funeral, the deceased's chopsticks are placed straight up in a bowl of uncooked rice at the altar and, after cremation, the deceased's bones are passed from chopstick to chopstick.) Finally, greedy eaters who are fed up with being underfed in Japan should resist the temptation to use the chopsticks as fishing rods to probe for and pinch the biggest morsels of food.

After mastering the rules, eaters are bound to find chopsticks terrifically tactile, sublimely simple, and fantastically functional. Connoisseurs appreciate the aesthetic pleasures of, say, pulling apart a pair of attached wooden chopsticks (listen for the satisfying "snap!") or putting rice to their lips with elegantly smooth, lacquered sticks. The utensils foster a sense of sharing by encouraging diners to serve themselves from communal plates. Chopsticks can also be more practical than the pedestrian knife and fork—for instance, long chopsticks are ideal for frying foods because they remove the chef from the line of fire of splattering hot oil.

Although the wooden sticks seem ingrained in Japanese culture, officials in the school lunch division of Japan's Ministry of Education are becoming concerned that Japanese young people, who are often weaned on non-chopstick-friendly fast food such as hot dogs and pizza, are forgetting (or never learning) how to wield the mighty sticks. As a result, some teachers and parents now encourage kids to practice with trainer chopsticks (designed with loops to mark the proper placement of fingers), study chopstick training videos, or even attend remedial chopstick classes.

Not everyone is a chopstick stickler, however. Some dentists claim that because food eaten with chopsticks is cut up into bite-size chunks, chopsticks are indirectly responsible for insufficient chewing, which leads to tooth decay. Moreover, environmental groups such as the Japan Tropical Forest Action Network have protested that the Japanese yearly use thirty billion disposable wooden chopsticks, or *waribashi* (literally, "splittable chopsticks"), at the expense of beleaguered Asian forests. Organizations such as the Society to Reconsider Waribashi and the Waribashi Action Network are encouraging eaters to dispense with the wasteful throwaway variety and bring their own reusable chopsticks when dining out. Bowing to environmental concerns, one major bank has banned the disposable sticks from its corporate cafeteria and invested in reusable plastic sticks and a chopstick washing machine. For their part, manufacturers of wooden chopsticks continue to defend the utensils as environmentally sound. Claiming that chopsticks are made from wood that is unfit for other purposes, they view any attempt to curb the use of disposable wooden chopsticks as the irrational demand of the ecological stick-in-the-mud.

In Japan, the ability to raise food to one's lips with two elongated sticks is a serious business since the prospect of malnutrition literally hangs in the balance. Diners who take a stab at this manner of eating and turn out to be all thumbs might remember the handy Japanese expression, *"Fooku kudasai."* Translation: "May I have a fork please?"

A Wrinkle out of Time

Kimono

Unlike some slouchy Westerners who routinely appear in oversized T-shirts and torn blue jeans, the Japanese take their fashion seriously. Depending on the occasion, dressing up in Japan may mean donning a dazzling designer dress, sporting a spiffy sports coat, or cloaking oneself in that classical courtly creation . . . the kimono.

Reflecting the Japanese appreciation for applied art, kimono are boldly shaped garments that delight with elegant embroidery. Usually draped over the wearer and tied with an *obi*, or sash, the versatile kimono is most often worn at New Year's, an adolescent's coming-of-age ceremony, and wedding parties. For formal events, ladies might appear in elaborate silk kimono embellished with classical motifs. For casual wear, both sexes turn to the *yukata*—wonderfully cool blue-and-white cotton kimono. (Yukata are often provided at Japanese inns for use strictly on the premises, so visitors should suppress any temptation to take them home as stolen souvenirs.) There are also dignified black kimono for funerals and wedding gown kimono as sumptuously intricate as the bride's own elaborately designed hair. The unwed tend to wear bright, long-sleeved kimono, while older, married ladies choose kimono with more subdued colors and shorter sleeves.

Finicky dressers who panic when fiddling with uncooperative hooks or buttons will find putting on a kimono a form of sartorial sadism. Just slipping into the one-size-fits-all body-length fabric, forming all the correct folds, and tying each kimono layer with a special belt can make one long for the Western corset, which seems almost comfortable and uncomplicated in contrast. In the old days, a Japanese girl's grandmother would teach her how to put on the kimono, but today, as extended families contract, kimono classes offer instruction on how to wear the ungainly garment. Top students may compete in the All Japan Kimono Contest, where they are judged on dressing technique, speed, and final appearance. For the unschooled, there are kimono dressing specialists. One "love hotel" even reportedly has a lady on staff to help kimono-clad lovers slip back into their clothes after a tryst.

Antique kimono may cost several thousand dollars, and standard silk models run about $1,500. Less expensive is the polyester variety, which would bring tears to the eyes of any self-respecting silk-weaver. Because kimono are worn relatively infrequently, cost-conscious Japanese are starting to rent rather than purchase the radiant robes. As a result, some kimono sales are sagging lower than hemlines.

Like so much in Japanese culture, kimono require painstaking precision and patience. Not only does weaving, wearing, airing, and refolding the traditional Japanese dress demand serious time and effort, but once harnessed in a kimono, one has limited options. Wrapped up like a walking Christmas parcel and stuffed into constricting footwear, the kimono wearer is constrained from moving forward quickly or beating a hasty retreat. Even for veterans of the All Japan Kimono Contest, this restriction on maneuverability is one wrinkle that is hard to iron out.

Strictly for Heels

KUTSU

shoes

Enter a Japanese home with *kutsu* (shoes) still on your feet and you commit the ultimate indiscretion. To the Japanese, wearing shoes indoors is a sure way to put your foot in your mouth.

Before stepping up into a house's *genkan*, or entryway, remove your shoes, place them neatly together facing the entrance and don house slippers provided by the hosts. Don't tread in a tatami (straw mat) room until you have left your footwear behind and are standing in your stockinged feet. A visit to the lavatory requires even more fancy footwork: park your house slippers outside the bathroom door and slip into special plastic or rubber shoes that have been laid out specially for the occasion. After leaving the john, remember to exchange the slippers; tracking toilet shoes through the house is strictly for heels.

Removing shoes is afoot almost everywhere in Japan—in inns, temples, gymnasiums, and even some pristine automobiles—so avoid wearing undarned, mismatching socks, or sneakers with lots of laces (only pros can slip in and out of those babies in a jiff). Those concerned about foot odor can tip-toe around this delicate problem by hiding the offending appendages under a low-heated table known as the *kotatsu*.

Padding around in slippers on Japan's cool, grainy wooden floors is a soothing textural sensation. It's also more hygienic than tracking dirt indoors with footwear, and, if nothing else, it lets cost-conscious consumers economize on doormats. Since most Japanese slippers are small, if you have big feet you should consider taking your own slippers to Japan. And while you're at it, make sure that they aren't too ungainly, or you'll risk sailing down Japan's steep, slippery stairways. The lesson here is clear: if the shoe fits. . . .

Making a Splash

FURO

bath

"*Furo, meshi, neru!*"—"Bath, food, and sleep!"— are said to be the three commands uttered by a demanding Japanese husband when he returns home from a hard day's work. Food and sleep are at times dispensable in Japan, but a *furo*, or bath, is always a must.

Ninety-five percent of Japanese have a bathtub at home, but unlike the elongated Western variety, Japanese tubs are squarish and squat, averaging five feet long, three feet wide, and two feet deep. Each person washes thoroughly outside the furo and then toe by toe gingerly submerges in the 104 degree water like a suicidal self-boiling egg. The water's numbing effect drains away the cares of the day, the sore muscles, the outside chill— just about everything, in fact, since one's body is effectively scalded into shock.

Since the bathwater is reused, the family member who takes the first bath enjoys the cleanest and hottest water and thus holds an esteemed position. Visitors who are

invited to stay the night at a Japanese home (a rare privilege, given the miniscule sizes of Japanese abodes) should therefore act duly appreciative if the host offers, "Won't you take a bath first?" (This is an honor, not a rude hint for scruffy guests.) Americans may complain that reusing the same bathtub water is unhygienic, but then the Japanese balk at the Western practice of washing one's body while inside (as opposed to outside) the tub and then soaking in the dirty water.

For the dwindling number of Japanese who lack a *furo* at home, there are traditional *sentoo* (literally "cash for hot water"), or communal public baths, where one can still enjoy talking over the day's events in an oversized tub together with one's naked neighbors. Armed with a handy plastic bucket, a bar of soap, and a tiny washcloth that also serves as a towel, the bather cheerfully flip-flops down the path to the local sentoo in his or her slippers. Parking all footwear in boxes outside the sentoo, he or she then passes through the sliding screens and pays the attendant who, like the umpire in a mixed-doubles tennis match, is perched unabashedly above the wall separating the sexes.

After undressing, the sentoo patron throws modesty to the wind (that tiny washcloth is not going to conceal much anyway), enters the tiled bathing chamber, and sits on a five-inch-high wooden stool in front of a mirror surrounded with hot and cold water spigots and a tiny shower nozzle. He or she then soaps up, scrubs down, and joins the others for a relaxing soak. Once in the tub, silent meditation is perfectly appropriate, but so is conversation. The Japanese say, "the relationship between naked people is an honest one." Even Japanese gangsters, who might prefer to bathe incognito, are exposed in the sentoo by their head-to-toe telltale tattoos.

With the increase in home furos, the emergence of "coin showers" (inexpensive twenty-four-hour rental showers), and skyrocketing real estate prices, sentoo owners are facing serious financial difficulties in trying to keep their heads above water. The number of sentoo in Tokyo has dried up from over 2,600 after the war to fewer than 1,900 today. The younger generation has become increasingly reluctant to bathe in the nude in public; breaching long-established etiquette, bashful youngsters now sometimes take to wearing bathing suits in the sentoo.

Desperate for customers, some of today's sentoo owners are trying to make a splash with customers by providing color television sets, video games, or, for the business bather, fax machines. Others have installed *harinoyu*, or "needle baths." These use underwater electric currents to jolt the skin—a relaxing treatment which, one hopes, stops short of turning the bather into toast. Recognizing the decline in public baths and reasoning that sentoo are, after all, a public service, the Japanese government has even begun to subsidize them with grants for remodeling and promotional activities.

Today, fewer Japanese may be patronizing sentoo, but they are increasingly spending vacation time at one of the nation's many luxurious *onsen*, or hot spring baths, usually located in resort towns. Onsen visitors disrobe, wash thoroughly, and then dunk in the medicinal salt and mineral waters. Once in the pool-sized tub, they may take deep breaths of the intoxicating sulfurous air or, if a more direct route to inebriation is preferred, indulge in long, slow sips of saké. Outdoor or semi-outdoor onsen give the "let's-commune-with-nature" types the chance to expose themselves on half-submerged rocks amid snow-covered pines.

For Westerners unschooled in the art of Japanese bathing, the ultimate *faux pas* is lathering up in the tub or pulling out the plug before others have had a chance to soak. In refining bathing etiquette, the Japanese have left one crucial question unanswered for big-boned foreigners who also want to take the plunge: how do you submerge your knees in a twenty-four-inch tub and then dry them off properly with a six-inch towel?

Braving the Indoor Wind-chill Factor

KOTATSU

low, heated table

For warm, cuddly coziness Japanese-style, nothing beats snuggling up at a *kotatsu*—a low, heated table draped with a long feather-stuffed comforter.

In Japan, where eighty percent of the population lacks centrally heated homes, family members brave winter's indoor wind-chill factor by huddling around their communal kotatsu, toasting their feet near the heating element under the table, and pulling up the thick feather comforter luxuriously around their waists. Stretching out under a kotatsu with a cup of saké or tea in one hand and a *mikan* (mandarin orange) in the other is, quite simply, bliss.

First popular in the mid-1950s, the kotatsu harks back to the medieval practice of covering burning charcoals with a table and quilt. In the modern-day kotatsu, electricity replaces charcoal, and the kotatsu comforter often has pockets for books, cigarettes, and, of course, the all-important television remote control. One new model, advertised as an "anti-odor kotatsu," even reportedly quells the smell of sweaty socks.

Since the kotatsu leaves the user exposed from the waist up, wearing plush quilted jackets has become a popular way to keep one's upper half as toasty as the bottom half. Bundled up like this, even the most stoic salaryman is likely to nod off right under the table. So comfortable is the kotatsu that it can make entire families think twice before getting up to answer either the phone or even the call of nature.

Some predict that if and when central heating becomes the norm, the kotatsu will be rendered obsolete. For kotatsu lovers, the demise of a device that encourages snuggling while warming both the heart and the toes is a truly chilling thought.

Afterword

My brother likes to say that a Westerner visiting Japan is perennially poor, hungry, and illiterate, and that the most satisfying view of the country is from the runway of Tokyo's Narita Airport as the plane lifts off to return to New York. I, for one, do not share this view. For me, every journey to Japan brings with it new and memorable experiences of a world far from my life in America, whether it be admiring the perfect geometry of a boxed lunch on a bullet train or soaking outdoors at night in a hot spring bath while it snows.

Writing this book has given me the chance to relive these and other experiences and to realize how attached I have become to Japan. This in spite of all the daily obstacles I encountered in trying to understand the country—struggling to find my way on unmarked Japanese streets, straining to memorize seemingly countless Japanese characters, and putting up with the waiter at the local coffee shop who insisted on serving me two coffees and a jelly doughnut even when I had clearly ordered (or at least thought I had ordered) two glazed doughnuts and a cup of tea.

And now for some advice to others who might wish to

follow in my footsteps:

* First, bring a soft pillow, since tatami floors are harder than you think.
* Second, bring a map written in English, because you're not going to find your way to the hotel with the directions the travel agent gave you in New York.
* Third, bring cold cash—not just credit cards or travelers checks, which only make the locals nervous.
* Fourth, bring antacid, because no matter how much soy sauce you pour on the raw squid, it's still raw squid.

And now for some don'ts:

* Don't wait for taxis to stop for you: they're in no rush to pick up foreigners, and you can use the exercise anyway.
* Don't wear toilet slippers outside the toilet, and don't wear shoes inside your room (but you have already learned this, right?)
* Don't convert dollars to yen in your head, since you might faint, or starve, or both.
* Don't try using irony on the Japanese: neither your Japanese nor their English is likely to be up to it, and it will only lead to ugly misunderstandings.
* Don't expect the Japanese to invite you to their homes, but be prepared to host them and each of their friends, relatives, and nodding acquaintances who will certainly visit you back in America.
* Finally, don't forget to go with a healthy sense of adventure, because you'll be able to dine out on your experiences for the rest of your life.

In the final analysis, from a foreigner's perspective, there is one true mark of the wonder of Japan: the irresistible urge we all feel to return.

Acknowledgments

I f ever a book was fun to write and illustrate, it is this discussion of the surprising ways and byways of Japan. This look at Japan from afar could not have been completed without the contributions of many friends, whose help I gratefully acknowledge: for introducing me to the different faces of Japan, Tobias Gruber, Miya and Akira Lippit, the Yoshii family, Kaoru Takada, Elizabeth Sweeney, Alice Young, and all my former colleagues at Nagashima & Ohno; for good ideas and other assistance, Mark Loughridge, Steven Lukow, and Yoichiro Taniguchi; for scrupulous reading of the manuscript in various stages, Kurt Mitchells, Gerhard Kallmann, John Kallmann, Carlos and Brigitte Palacios, Deborah Devedjian, Rachel Wagner, David Kissinger, Eva Tan, Stephen DeCosse, and Kyoko Maeda; for invaluable advice about the practicalities of publishing, Naoko Tsunoi, Michael Schelp, Michael Lynton, and Lili and David Smilow; for faith in the project and moral support, Younghee and Bruce Ottley, Ruth Mitchells, Raffael and Janna Jovine, Janet Koplos, Yuriko and Neil Gross, Nozomu Nakaoka, and Mark and Anna Elliott; and for unstinting encouragement and cheerful guidance, my editor, Barry Lancet. Above all, I acknowledge my family, Marlies K. Danziger, Thomas C.

Danziger, and Susan V. Danziger, whose enthusiasm and affectionate criticism kept me firmly focused on the serious business of taking a lighthearted look at Japan.